DANIEL

DANIEL

By

G. COLEMAN LUCK

MOODY PRESS

CHICAGO

ISBN: 0-8024-2027-3

Printed in the United States of America

CONTENTS

CHAPTER   PAGE

	Introduction—Background	7
	Outline of the Book	15
1	The King's Food and the Faithful Hebrew Youths	21
2	Nebuchadnezzar's Dream of the Great Image	31
3	The Faithful Jews in the Fiery Furnace	46
4	The Humbling of Nebuchadnezzar	57
5	Belshazzar and the Handwriting on the Wall	65
6	Daniel in the Lions' Den	73
7	The Vision of the Four Beasts and the Little Horn	83
8	The Vision of the Ram and the Rough Goat	92
9	Daniel's Prayer and the Vision of the Seventy Weeks	98
10	The Vision of the Glory of God	107
11	Prophecies Concerning Persia, Grecia and the Time of the End	112
12	The Great Tribulation and the Resurrection	121
	Bibliography	125

Introduction

BACKGROUND

THE PROPHET

THE BOOK OF DANIEL is outstanding in two ways. It contains clear revelation concerning some of the greatest themes of prophecy, and at the same time has many inspiring and helpful lessons for the practical life of the Christian. A close study of this book will provide nourishing spiritual food for any Christian, and its teachings are essential to an understanding of prophetic truth.

The first item of interest to us in connection with any worthwhile book is *the author*. The real Author of this book, as of other books of the Bible, was the Holy Spirit of God (II Tim. 3:16; II Peter 1:21). But on the human side, who was the channel that God used for the production of this portion of Scripture? It was written by Daniel the prophet, an Israelite who lived approximately from 618-534 B.C. Thus it will be seen that the life span of this man was around eighty-four years. He lived in momentous times— during the reigns of such great kings as Nebuchadnezzar of Babylon and Cyrus the Persian. Further Old Testament mention of the man Daniel is to be found in the book of Ezekiel, who was in part contemporary with him. In Ezekiel 14:14, 20, Daniel is classed with Noah and Job as being one of the *godliest* of men. In Ezekiel 28:3 he is referred to as one of the *wisest* of men. This description fits perfectly the character of Daniel as pictured in his own book. It may be said in passing, that there are two other Daniels mentioned in the Old Testament—one a son of David (I Chron. 3:1), the other a descendant of Aaron who was associated with Ezra and Nehemiah in the rebuilding of Jerusalem (Ezra 8:2; Neh. 10:6). These were other men by the same name, who had no connection with the Daniel with whom we are now concerned.

From earliest times until the seventeenth century of our era, it was generally accepted that this Daniel was the author of the book bearing his name. During all these hundreds of years apparently only one voice of importance was raised against this view—that of Porphyry, a Greek nonchristian philosopher who lived in the third century A.D. However with the rise of English deism in the seventeenth century (a movement which accepted the existence of God but rejected the Christian faith and the Bible as the revelation of God) this view was challenged. From that time to the present, so-called liberal scholars have denied the genuineness of the book: "The great majority of critics regard this book as entirely spurious and composed centuries after the death of the sixth century Daniel. They understand it to be a work of historical fiction composed about 165 B.C. and intended to encourage the resistance movement against the tyranny of Antiochus Epiphanes."[1] Arguments for this position revolve largely around four features: (1) the predictions, (2) the miracles, (3) the language, and (4) the historical statements.

(1) "Champions of the Maccabean date theory allege

[1]Gleason L. Archer, Jr., *A Survey of Old Testament Introduction*, p. 368.

that it was impossible for a sixth century author to have composed such detailed predictions concerning coming events in the history of Israel as are contained in the prophetic chapters of the book of Daniel."[2] But is it not true that those who reject *the predictions* do so largely because they reject prophecy as such? They feel that the predictions concerning the various world empires are so minutely accurate that they must have been written *after* rather than *before* the events described. Their position is really not only a denial of the Bible but of theism itself (the belief in a personal God). If there is a sovereign, omniscient God, He has the power to predict the future, and in minute detail if He wishes to do so. (2) As for *the miracles* such as those of the fiery furnace and the lions' den, there is nothing incongruous or grotesque about them; and if books of the Bible are to be rejected because they contain accounts of wonderful miracles, then we must discard practically the whole Bible. (3) Regarding *the language,* it is claimed that since there are three Greek words for musical instruments and a number of Persian words, this means that the book must have been written *after* the Persian and Greek empires, and that therefore the supposed prophecies are merely past history written as if it were prophecy. However, we now know that there were Greek captives in Nineveh as early as 700 B.C., and such a king as Nebuchadnezzar could easily have procured Greek musical instruments. Many of the words previously thought to be Persian have now proved to be Babylonian in origin. Most of the words the critics refer to are titles, names of clothing, and other technical terms that could easily have passed from Media to Babylon in Daniel's time. Also since Daniel did not

[2]Archer, p. 381.

complete his book until the Persian Empire had been in power for several years, it seems quite reasonable that he might have used Persian governmental terms, then current, even in portions of his history which related to his youth.[3] (4) As to *historical statements,* a few apparent difficulties along this line can be fairly easily explained, and are dealt with later in the exposition of the book. Dr. Robert Dick Wilson, one of the greatest Hebrew scholars of this century, shows the fallacy of such objections in an article on this subject which interested readers can consult.[4]

On the other hand, it should be noted that there is positive evidence that Daniel did write this book as and when claimed. The apocryphal book of I Maccabees (written about 135 B.C.) refers to Daniel as an accredited book. The Septuagint Greek Version of the Old Testament, translated between 280 and 180 B.C., contains the book of Daniel. We know from Josephus that the Jews of Christ's day recognized Daniel as the author and his book as canonical. Josephus tells us that Alexander the Great marched on Jerusalem to punish the Jews for their loyalty to Darius, but Jaddua the high priest (Neh. 12:11, 22) met him at the head of a procession and averted his wrath by showing him the prophecy of Daniel, which foretold that a Grecian king would overthrow Persia (Dan. 8:1-7, 20-21).[5] This happened in 322 B.C. Alexander was indeed unusually favorable to the Jews after this time, and the statement of Josephus accounts for his favor.

Most important of all, the book of Daniel is alluded to a number of times in the New Testament. Notice especially

[3]For a fuller, more satisfying discussion of this matter see Archer, pp. 374-76.
[4]Robert Dick Wilson, in *International Standard Bible Encyclopaedia,* ed. James Orr, II, 5785-86.
[5]Josephus, *Antiquities of the Jews,* XI. 8. 4-5.

Matthew 24:15. In this verse from the great Olivet discourse our Lord Jesus Christ mentions certain things "spoken of by Daniel the prophet." A similar statement is found in Mark 13:14.[6] Thus our Lord, who said, "I am the truth," bears testimony to the fact that Daniel actually *lived*, that he was a *prophet*, that he wrote the book attributed to him, and that he prophesied events which were *still future* at the time Christ spoke.

PURPOSE OF THE BOOK

The next question of practical interest concerns the *purpose* of the book. In this connection the relation of the various prophetic books to each other should be noted. A long-used method of dividing the prophetic books of the Old Testament is simply by length, placing them in two classes—Major and Minor Prophets. The Major Prophets include Isaiah, Jeremiah and Ezekiel. The Minor Prophets comprise Hosea through Malachi. Some doubt arises as to which group Daniel should be placed in. Usually it has been included with the Major Prophets.[7] This method of division is not chronological, and in some ways is unsatisfactory, but it does have its helpful features.

Dr. G. Campbell Morgan points out the fact that, generally speaking, the four Major Prophets give the unveiling of the *King;* the twelve Minor Prophets, the unveiling of the *kingdom.*[8] It is interesting to notice some contrasts between the four Major Prophets. As to the time of writing,

---

[6]The ASV omits the phrase in Mark's gospel, but retains it in Matthew's.

[7]Chapterwise Hosea is longer than Daniel, 14 to 12. Versewise, however, Daniel has 357 to Hosea's 197, and has many more words: 11,606 to 5,175 (in the AV).

[8]G. Campbell Morgan, *Living Messages of the Books of the Bible, Old Testament*, II, 148.

Isaiah ministered more than a hundred years before the
Babylonian exile, when Judah was relatively prosperous.
Jeremiah labored during the turbulent reign of Judah's last
kings. Ezekiel prophesied to a group of exiles in captivity
in Babylon. Daniel ministered not directly to Israel at all
but in the midst of the great world powers of Babylon and
Medo-Persia.

Likewise it is of interest to compare the central revelation of each of these four writers. Isaiah's supreme revelation is that of the throne of Jehovah, particularly in relation
to God's sovereignty and grace (Isa. 6:5). Jeremiah reveals
the activity of Jehovah in connection with sin. In his book
we see God judging sin, suffering because of sin, and finally
victorious over sin. Ezekiel presents the person of Jehovah.
He shows His supremacy over man, His service for man,
and His revelation of Himself to man, in spite of which
revelation there still remains much mystery about His person (see chap. 1). Daniel's supreme revelation is that of
God's continuous control over the whole earth as He fulfills the purpose of His grace. Morgan aptly says: "In
Daniel we have the revelation of the power and wisdom of
the Lord God in the government of the world to the end
of the days."[9]

As a further simple comparison, Isaiah enunciates the
principles of divine government, Jeremiah depicts the *practice* of divine government, Ezekiel portrays the *person* of
the Governor, and Daniel reveals the *persistence* of His
government.

Robert Dick Wilson has given an excellent summary in
the following cogent words:

[9]*Ibid.*, p. 151.

The book is not intended to give an account of the life of Daniel. It gives neither his lineage, nor his age, and recounts but a few of the events of his long career. Nor is it meant to give a record of the history of Israel during the exile, nor even of the captivity in Babylon. Its purpose is to show how by His providential guidance, His miraculous interventions, His foreknowledge and almighty power, the God of heaven controls and directs the forces of Nature and the history of nations, the lives of Hebrew captives and of the mightiest of the kings of the earth, for the accomplishment of His divine and beneficent plans for His servants and people.[10]

The basic message of the book deals with that period which our Lord called "the times of the Gentiles" (Luke 21:24). In the words of Dr. Louis Talbot, Daniel contains the revelation of "the commencement, the character, the course and the consummation of 'the times of the Gentiles.' "

The book of Daniel is quite easy to outline in a simple way. It contains two principal divisions: history (chaps. 1-6) and prophecy (chaps. 7-12).[11] The sections have truly been called "The Historic Night" and "The Prophetic Light."[12] In the historical section, *chapter 1* concerns the king's food and the faithful Hebrew youths. *Chapter 2* gives Nebuchadnezzar's dream of the great image. *Chapter*

[10]Wilson, p. 784.

[11]It is understood of course that the first six chapters are not devoid of prophecy. Chap. 2 contains one of the greatest prophecies of the entire Bible. The last six chapters on the other hand include various historical allusions. However the first half of the book is presented as and is largely devoted to history, while the last half relates four great prophetic visions granted to Daniel. The division is very obvious since chaps. 1-6 proceed in chronological order, while chap. 7 suddenly goes back in time to a date shortly prior to the events of chap. 5. The four visions are then given in their own chronological order.

[12]Morgan, II, 144.

3 recounts the story of the faithful Jews in the fiery furnace. *Chapter 4* depicts the humbling of the proud Nebuchadnezzar. *Chapter 5* tells of King Belshazzar and the handwriting on the wall. In *chapter 6* we have the familiar but ever thrilling record of Daniel in the lions' den.

The strictly prophetic section opens with Daniel's vision of the four beasts and the little horn in *chapter 7*. Then follows the vision of the ram and the rough goat in *chapter 8*. The great prayer of Daniel in *chapter 9* finds its answer in the vision of the seventy weeks. *Chapters 10-12* relate the final vision given to Daniel. *Chapter 10* introduces this vision and pictures the glory of God. *Chapter 11* contains detailed prophecies concerning Persia, Grecia and the time of the end. *Chapter 12* concludes this grand prophecy with facts concerning the great tribulation and the resurrection.

OUTLINE OF THE BOOK

I. HISTORICAL SECTION ("The Historic Night") (1:1—6:28)

    A. The King's Food and the Faithful Hebrew Youths (1:1-21)

        1. The Fall of Jerusalem (1:1-2)

        2. Hebrew Youths Selected for Special Training (1:3-5)

        3. Daniel and His Friends (1:6-7)

        4. Daniel's Purpose and the Test (1:8-14)

        5. Result of the Test (1:15-17)

        6. The Presentation Before the King (1:18-21)

    B. Nebuchadnezzar's Dream of the Great Image (2:1-49)

        1. The Forgotten Dream (2:1-13)

        2. The Interpreter Found (2:14-30)

        3. The Dream and Its Interpretation Given (2:31-45)

        4. The Aftermath (2:46-49)

    C. The Faithful Jews in the Fiery Furnace (3:1-30)

        1. Nebuchadnezzar's Image Worship (3:1-7)

        2. The Faithful Jews Accused (3:8-12)

        3. The Faithful Jews Refuse To Worship the Image (3:13-18)

        4. The Faithful Jews Cast into the Fiery Furnace (3:19-23)

        5. The Faithful Jews Delivered and Honored (3:24-30)

D. The Humbling of Nebuchadnezzar (4:1-37)
  1. Preface to Nebuchadnezzar's Proclamation (4:1-3)
  2. Nebuchadnezzar's Dream of the Great Tree (4:4-18)
  3. The Dream Interpreted by Daniel (4:19-27)
  4. The Dream Fulfilled and Its Result (4:28-37)
E. Belshazzar and the Handwriting on the Wall (5:1-31)
  1. Belshazzar's Feast and His Defiance of Jehovah (5:1-4)
  2. The Handwriting on the Wall (5:5-9)
  3. Daniel Brought Before the King (5:10-16)
  4. Daniel's Interpretation (5:17-29)
  5. The Aftermath (5:30-31)
F. Daniel in the Lions' Den (6:1-28)
  1. Daniel's Position Under Darius (6:1-3)
  2. Daniel's Enemies and Their Plot Against Him (6:4-9)
  3. Daniel's "Obedient Disobedience" (6:10-15)
  4. Daniel's Punishment and His Deliverance (6:16-24)
  5. Darius' Proclamation (6:25-28)
II. PROPHETICAL SECTION ("The Prophetic Light") (7:1—12:13)
  A. The Vision of the Four Beasts and the Little Horn (7:1-28)
    1. Daniel's Vision (7:1-14)
    2. The Interpretation (7:15-28)
  B. The Vision of the Ram and the Rough Goat (8:1-27)
    1. Daniel's Vision (8:1-14)
    2. The Interpretation (8:15-27)
  C. Daniel's Prayer and the Vision of the Seventy Weeks (9:1-27)
    1. Daniel's Prayer (9:1-19)
    2. The Vision of the Seventy Weeks (9:20-27)

D. The Vision of the Glory of God (10:1-21)
  1. Vision of the Preincarnate Christ (10:1-9)
  2. Angelic Ministry (10:10-14)
  3. Divine Ministry (10:15-17)
  4. Introduction to the Final Prophecy (10:18-21)
E. Prophecies Concerning Persia, Grecia and the Time of the End (11:1-45)
  1. Prophecies Concerning Persia (11:1-2)
  2. Prophecies Concerning Grecia (11:3-4)
  3. Prophecies Concerning Two Branches of the Divided Greek Empire: Syria and Egypt (11:5-35)
  4. The Time of the End—The Antichrist (11:36-45)
F. The Great Tribulation and the Resurrection (12:1-13)
  1. The Great Tribulation (12:1)
  2. The Resurrection (12:2-3)
  3. Epilogue (12:4-13)

PART ONE
HISTORICAL SECTION
(1:1—6:28)

1

THE KING'S FOOD AND THE FAITHFUL
HEBREW YOUTHS

(1:1-21)

THE FALL OF JERUSALEM (1:1-2)

THERE WERE EVIDENTLY three deportations of the Jews to
Babylon. According to these verses, Daniel and his three
friends were taken captive in the first deportation, which
took place about 606 B.C. (II Kings 24:1). At that time
Nebuchadnezzar took the vessels from the house of God to
the temple in Babylon. The second deportation occurred
about 598 B.C., eight years after Daniel went to Babylon.
This occurred after Jehoiachin, the son of Jehoiakim, had
reigned only three months (II Kings 24:8-16). Ezekiel was
carried into captivity at that time.[1] The third and final
deportation, together with the destruction of Jerusalem itself, came to pass in 588 B.C. in the eleventh year of King
Zedekiah, who was the brother of Jehoiakim and the uncle
of Jehoiachin (II Kings 25:8-12; II Chron. 36:20).

All this was the fulfillment of prophecy previously given.
From such passages as Jeremiah 25:1-4 and II Chronicles

[1]It is presumed that Ezekiel was carried into captivity along with Jehoiachin, since his book begins with him already in Babylon, and he dates
all of his prophecies according to the "year of king Jehoiachin's captivity"
(Ezek. 1:1-2; 8:1; 20:1; 26:1; 29:1; 29:17; 40:1; et al.).

21

36:14-21, it will be seen that the captivity was a direct judgment of God on the nation Israel, because of her terrible sins, particularly idolatry, failure to observe the Sabbatic years of rest, and refusal to heed the faithful warning of God's prophets. Jehovah, in His mercy, allowed the Israelites to go on for a considerable time in their sins, but finally the time of His patience came to an end and judgment descended.

A weekly newspaper in the Middle West once printed the letter of an atheist who, to disprove the beliefs of his Christian neighbors, had devoted a certain portion of his land to corn, doing every bit of work on this section on Sunday. "And now," he wrote, "I find that in September I have more bushels of corn per acre on that part of my land worked exclusively on Sunday than my neighbors have on their land, which they did not work on Sunday. Doesn't that prove that there is no God?" The editor's answer was brief but to the point. "No," he wrote, "that does not prove there is no God. It simply proves that God does not always settle His accounts in September!" God hates sin, and if He permits it to go unchecked for awhile it is simply to give the sinner every opportunity to repent. But remember that there will eventually be a day of accounting for all who persist in evil, even as there was a terrible day of reckoning for Israel (cf. Rom. 2:3-6).

HEBREW YOUTHS SELECTED FOR
SPECIAL TRAINING (1:3-5)

Ashpenaz, the king's chief chamberlain,[2] received a spe-

---

[2]The Hebrew word here rendered "eunuch" is *saris*. According to William Gesenius it refers in its primary meaning to "one castrated . . . such as the Eastern kings were accustomed to set over the care of their women" (*Hebrew and Chaldee Lexicon to the Old Testament Scriptures*, trans. Samuel P. Tragelles, p. 595). It seems that this evil practice, which be-

cial order from Nebuchadnezzar. He was told to select certain Jewish boys, young fellows probably around the age of twelve or fourteen.[3] They were to be boys of noble birth, and also of attractive personal appearance. In addition, they were to be youths with something *inside* their heads as well as on the *outside*—good students already well trained, and possessing the ability to go on in further education at Babylon.

For these young men the king made very gracious provision. They were to be taught the learning of the Chal-

came widespread in the East and has not been unknown even in the Western world, was fostered by the jealousy of kings who feared to let normal males serve in their harems and so caused their emasculation. Such desexed persons were also valued for duty elsewhere as they "were considered remarkable for their fidelity to their masters" (Gesenius), a supposition which it is very doubtful that history would substantiate. Authorities seem to agree however that the term *saris* and its Greek counterpart *eunouchos* "were sometimes applied to those filling important posts, without regard to corporeal mutilation" (Merrill F. Unger, *Unger's Bible Dictionary*, p. 328). Gesenius gives as a secondary meaning of the word: "any minister of the court, although not castrated; although it is difficult to determine in what places the primary meaning of the word is preserved, and in what it is lost." Possibly the AV translators had this in mind when they not only rendered *saris* by the word "eunuch" some 17 times in the Old Testament, but in addition rendered it 13 times "officer" and 12 times "chamberlain." It seems probable that in Daniel 1:3 the term is to be taken in its secondary sense rather than the primary, and that Ashpenaz was simply the chief of all the palace officials. It has even been conjectured by some (e.g., Clarence Larkin, *The Book of Daniel*, p. 22) that Daniel himself and his friends were in this manner mutilated (based especially on the prophecy in Isaiah 39:7) but this is very doubtful to say the least.

[3]Robert Jamieson, A. R. Fausset, and David Brown, *A Commentary on the Old and New Testaments*, IV, 383. As to the age of these young men there is much difference of opinion among commentators, however. Keil says "fifteen to twenty" (*Biblical Commentary on the Book of Daniel*, p. 73). Thomson judges that "sixteen to eighteen seems the lowest limit we can set" (as quoted in *Pulpit Commentary*, XIII, 13). Larkin says "about twenty" (*The Book of Daniel*, p. 23). The Hebrew word used in Daniel 1:3, *yeled*, is indefinite. It simply means a "born one" and is used of an infant (Isaac, Gen. 21:8) as well as of "the young men that were grown up" with Rehoboam, at the time he was forty-one years of age (II Kings 12:8; 14:21). Daniel and his friends, at the time they were taken captive, were obviously quite young and yet were by no means tiny children as their qualifications clearly show.

deans,[4] and during this period of instruction were to be
provided with food from the king's own table. They were
to receive a "college education," so to speak, with all ex-
penses paid. Why did the king go to all this trouble and
expense? These men were to be thoroughly prepared so
that at the end of three years of study "they might stand
before the king." This was not simply that he might behold their personal beauty, but rather that he might profit
from the wise advice they would be able to give. In spite
of all his faults, Nebuchadnezzar had many kingly qualities.
He realized the great responsibility that was his in the
government of his vast new empire, and he wanted the best
of counselors, not even scorning men of other nations than
his own. Matthew Henry has well written: "He did not,
like Ahasuerus [of the book of Esther] appoint them to
choose him out young women for the service of his lusts,
but young men for the service of his government."[5]

DANIEL AND HIS FRIENDS (1:6-7)

For the first time, four of the Hebrew youths are now
introduced by name. There is no indication as to the total
number of boys chosen, but evidently there were a good
many. From this large number these four stand out. The
rest are now forgotten. In no library on earth can their
names be found, or even their total number. But Daniel
and his three friends still bear a living testimony. Why?
Because even in a day when everything seemed against
them, and there were apparently no human helpers to
whom they could turn, nevertheless they were determined

[4]Chaldea was "originally a small territory in southern Babylonia at the
head of the Persian Gulf, but later . . . the term came to include practically all of Babylonia . . ." (Unger, p. 187).
[5]Matthew Henry, *Commentary on the Whole Bible*, IV, 1018.

that they would be faithful to God, and obedient to His will regardless of the cost. "Only one life, 'twill soon be past; only what's done for Christ will last." So today the lives that really count are not those that merely go along with the crowd, but those who are determined to stand for Christ regardless of what the crowd does. Always remember that one plus God is a majority!

The fact that these four boys were from the tribe of Judah and of noble lineage is another striking fulfillment of prophecy—the prediction made to Hezekiah after his foolish display of pride (see Isa. 39:5-7).

The names of the four youths are significant. Daniel means "God is my judge."[6] That name truly typified the character of its possessor. Daniel was always conscious of being in the presence of Jehovah God—the great Judge of all the earth—and he was determined to please Him no matter what human judges might think.

Hananiah means "whom Jehovah hath favored." Mishael means literally "who is what God is?" This conveys the idea "who is comparable to God?" Azariah means "whom Jehovah helps."[7] Surely godly parents must have named these lads. Here is proof of the truthfulness of the promise "Train up a child in the way he should go: and when he is old, he will not depart from it" (Prov. 22:6). Though these boys were in a heathen land far from home, yet they did not forget the God whom their parents had taught them to know and honor.

As might be expected, these names did not please the prince of the eunuchs, who proceeded to confer new ones on Daniel and his companions. Daniel himself was named

---

[6]Unger, p. 237.
[7]Jamieson, Fausset and Brown, IV, 384.

Belteshazzar, which means "Bel's prince." Bel was one of
the heathen gods worshiped by the Babylonians. Hananiah
was given the name of Shadrach ("inspired by the sun-
god"). Mishael's name was changed to Meshach ("who is
comparable to Shak?" the name under which the Babylonians worshiped the goddess Venus). Azariah was named
Abed-nego ("servant of the shining fire," an allusion to the
fire-god).[8] From these new names it is easy to detect that
the prince was an idolater who cared nothing for the true
God; indeed the very name of the Lord Jehovah was evidently distasteful to him. This fact makes even more miraculous the working of God in such a man's heart so as to
cause him to have tender love for godly Daniel.

DANIEL'S PURPOSE AND THE TEST (1:8-14)

Daniel 1:8 is one of the truly great verses of the entire
Bible. A life devoted to God begins with *purpose of heart.*
If the child of God has from the very beginning such purpose of heart, then when tests come he will be ready, by
God's help, to stand for Him. Doubtless this is why some
believers fail in the hour of testing. There was not a previous determination to do the will of God regardless of the
cost.

Evidently this conviction originated with Daniel, but
when he revealed it to his friends, the three determined to
stand with him. The faithful life of an earnest believer
can be a source of great encouragement to others.

It is specifically stated that Daniel purposed not to defile
himself. His masters could change Daniel's name but not
his nature. Though far from his own land and in a heathen
idolatrous country, he nevertheless determined to maintain

[8]*Ibid.*

his separation unto God. While this aspect is not the whole, it is nevertheless an important part of the life of a child of God. Psalm 1 first speaks of what the blessed, or happy, man does not do, and then of what he does do. Many other Scripture passages do the same. There are evidently both negative and positive sides to the Christian life. There are certain things the believer should do if he is faithful to God; there are other things he should not do. Modern Christians are in a way also living in the midst of a Babylon (or Babel) —the present world system. Let all who know Him purpose, like Daniel, not to defile themselves with the sinful, or even with the questionable, things of this world (II Cor. 6:17-18). A husband dressing for an important engagement called to his wife, "Dear, what about this shirt I wore the other night? Is it clean enough to wear again?" "What do you think about it?" was her reply. "I'm not quite sure," he answered. The wife's conclusion then was "If it's doubtful, it's dirty." Surely this is good advice for judging actions as well as shirts.

It is further stated that Daniel determined not to defile himself with the king's meat and wine. The Jews had strict dietary laws. Possibly Daniel knew that swine's flesh or the flesh of things strangled would be offered to him (cf. Acts 15:20). Authorities tell us that usually such meat was also dedicated first of all to an idol. Many Christians in New Testament days felt that such meat would be defiling (I Cor. 8:4-13).[9] As for wine, many warnings against it are to be found in the Old Testament, particularly in the book of Proverbs, which was written long before Daniel's time. Daniel determined to "look not upon the wine when it is red" (Prov. 23:31). Possibly Daniel had taken the vows of

[9]H. D. M. Spence and Joseph S. Exell (eds.), *Pulpit Commentary*, XIII, 18.

a Nazarite (see Num. 6) which required abstinence from both "wine and strong drink."

Sometimes Christians seeking to live separated lives for God unfortunately seem to parade their holiness in a Pharisaical way before the world. Daniel was not like this. Although his own mind was quite settled, he did not present his position to his superior in proud self-righteous arrogance, but courteously and humbly made his request. Christians should ever be careful not to display a repellent "holier than thou" attitude with regard to their separation from worldly things.

When men make a stand for God, then He works for them (I Sam. 2:30). Daniel was a fine boy of lovable character. But that in itself was not enough and might indeed have merely antagonized this idolatrous prince. Verse 9 makes it clear that it was not Daniel's character that produced the result, but God's mysterious working. He can turn even the hearts of unsaved men in order to work out His own purposes. However through fear Ashpenaz objected to Daniel's request. But in the end he granted it. Surely God was dealing with this man's heart!

A new character is now mentioned (v. 11). Melzar means "steward" or "butler" (ASV) and is probably a title rather than an actual name. Melzar was the one who brought the food to the young men. Daniel asked this man for a test—that he and his three friends be allowed to eat pulse (ASV margin, "herbs"; the original word signifies vegetable food in general) [10] and drink water for ten days, instead of partaking of the king's meat and wine. It is not likely Melzar would have agreed to this proposition if Ashpenaz had not been favorable to it.

[10]Unger, p. 1143.

The Result of the Test (1:15-17)

At the end of the ten-day period, Daniel and his friends were found to be "fairer and fatter" than all their comrades. "This was in part a natural effect of their temperance, but it must be ascribed to the special blessing of God, which will make a little go a great way, a dinner of herbs better than a stalled ox."[11] From this time on no question was raised and the four friends were allowed to choose their own diet.

Their attainments were mental as well as physical (v. 17). Surely Daniel and his three companions applied themselves diligently to their studies, but again the result is ascribed to God. Even if native abilities bring us success, let us always remember that it is God who gives us these talents and the power to use them (James 1:17; I Cor. 4:7). Daniel, like Joseph of old, was also given the ability to interpret dreams and visions (Gen. 40-41). This "double portion" he probably received because he was the leader of the little group. This ability was to play an important part in his life in the days to come.

The Presentation Before the King (1:18-21)

The closing scene of the chapter takes the reader forward three years in time to the presentation before the king. At the end of the prescribed course of study, the king personally examined the entire group of young men with regard to "all matters of wisdom and understanding." Nebuchadnezzar must have been a man of real learning to have possessed the ability to question these scholarly boys so carefully. He did not bring them to Babylon in order that they might amuse him with entertaining stories. He was not

[11]Henry, p. 1020.

looking for jesters but for wise counselors; he was searching not for wit but for wisdom. A great nation is fortunate when it has leaders who seek out such assistance. In this examination Daniel and his friends not only excelled their own companions, but were "ten times better" than all the magicians and astrologers who were supposedly the wisest men in the realm. Again is the eternal principle illustrated that God honors those who honor Him (I Sam. 2:30).

Daniel and his three friends in chapter 1 have been thought to be a type of the faithful portion of Israel during the yet future great tribulation. Daniel 1 may possibly provide somewhat of an illustration of this still future period, but that it is a divinely intended type is highly questionable.[12] When the beast-king of the last days (directly foretold in Dan. 7 ff.) arises on the earth demanding divine worship for himself (II Thess. 2:3-4, *et al.*), there will be faithful Israelites like these four young friends who will refuse to defile themselves, but will instead courageously bear witness to the true God during those awful days (Dan. 7:25; Rev. 7:1-8; 14:1-5). Many details of this tribulation period are revealed by Daniel in later chapters of his book.

The statement that "Daniel continued even unto the first year of king Cyrus," with which the chapter closes, does not mean that this was the final year of Daniel's life, as one might hastily conclude since the date of his final vision is "the third year of Cyrus" (10:1). Apparently the thought is that Daniel held public office until the first year of Cyrus' reign. At that time the venerable old man "retired," so to speak.

---

[12]A. C. Gaebelein, *The Prophet Daniel*, p. 14.

2

NEBUCHADNEZZAR'S DREAM OF THE GREAT IMAGE

(2:1-49)

THE FORGOTTEN DREAM (2:1-13)

THIS CHAPTER CONTAINS one of the great key prophecies of the entire Bible—Nebuchadnezzar's dream of the great image. It is of such significance that it has sometimes been called "the *ABC* of prophecy."[1] The date with which the chapter opens provides something of a problem. Earlier we were told that the Hebrew youths were trained by the king for *three* years (1:5). Those years have evidently been completed at the time chapter 2 commences, yet we are now informed that it is but the *second* year of the reign of Nebuchadnezzar. How can this apparent discrepancy be explained? Simply thus: Nebuchadnezzar reigned first as subordinate to his father, Nabopolassar. Chapter 1 derives its date from that rule. The dating of chapter 2 refers to the period of his sole sovereignty.[2] "The very difficulty is a proof of genuineness: all was clear to the writer and the original readers, from their knowledge of the circumstances,

[1]H. A. Ironside, *Lectures on Daniel the Prophet*, p. 25.
[2]John W. Haley, *An Examination of the Alleged Discrepancies of the Bible*, p. 402.

and so he adds no explanation. A forger would not intro-
duce difficulties; the author did not *then* see any difficulty
in the case."[3] While Nebuchadnezzar was in Judaea his
father died, and then he himself became full king.

There came a night when this great king did not rest
well. He "dreamed dreams, wherewith his spirit was troubled, and his sleep brake from him" (v. 1). He did not
then realize it, but God was dealing with him. Many years
later King Ahasuerus of Persia had a somewhat similar experience (Esther 6:1). He was unable to sleep, and because of this heaven-sent insomnia, he began a random
investigation of court records which started the process that
eventually resulted in the temporal salvation of the whole
Jewish nation from its cruel enemy Haman. These are
instances of the unseen but mighty power of our God as
He works out His wonderful plans.

Later in the present chapter (v. 29) the experience of
Nebuchadnezzar leading up to his amazing dream is related. As he lay upon his bed in those few moments before
sleep came, he began to think of the fact that some day his
own life would inevitably end, and his curiosity was aroused
as to what would take place on the earth after he had passed
from the scene. The One who alone can reveal secrets gave
an answer to Nebuchadnezzar's curiosity. He, the first of
the great world monarchs, was given a glimpse of the entire course of that extensive period which Christ calls "the
times of the Gentiles" (Luke 21:24). This epoch Nebuchadnezzar saw, from his own reign down to the second
coming and personal rule of the Lord Jesus Christ. After
this experience, he awoke, but as can well be imagined, had
difficulty returning to sleep. He realized that something

[3]Jamieson, Fausset and Brown, *Commentary*, IV, 386.

out of the ordinary had happened, that this was no common dream. He felt certain that there was an important meaning, so he immediately sought to discover this secret.

His magicians were summoned. These men made great pretense of interpreting dreams, preparing horoscopes, and in various ways attempting to reveal secret things and forecast the future.[4] Probably they were at first highly pleased at the summons, thinking that some pretended "interpretation" could be given that would satisfy the king and obtain his favor. If so, they were soon sadly disillusioned.

In terse words the king explained his situation to his wise men. He had forgotten the dream but was sure he could recognize it if it were described to him. Again the hand of God is to be observed at work. He can take things out of minds as well as put them in. Why, it may be asked, did God give Nebuchadnezzar this miraculous dream and then cause him to immediately forget it? It is soon seen that God had a definite purpose in this as in all His dealings.

The magicians were ordered by the king to describe the dream and to supply the interpretation. If successful, great reward was promised them. For failure, terrible punishment was threatened.

As the Chaldeans answered the king, Daniel tells us that they spoke in "Syriack." At this point the language of the original text changes from Hebrew to Aramaic (Hebrew *aramith*). Aram is an ancient Bible name for Syria, taken from the Syrians' progenitor, a son of Shem (see Gen. 10:22-23). Aramaic is one of a number of related languages called by scholars Semitic. "North Semitic embraces the Aramaic family, which is usually divided into eastern and western branches . . . the western being the

[4]Merrill F. Unger, *Unger's Bible Dictionary*, pp. 187-88.

basis for Biblical Aramaic as found in Daniel and Ezra . . .
Hebrew and Moabite are dialects" of West Semitic.[5] While
Hebrew and Aramaic have similarities, being members of a
family, there are also numerous differences.

It is directly stated that the Chaldeans used this language in answering Nebuchadnezzar. However it is at first
surprising to find that after having written the preceding
material in Hebrew, Daniel quotes the actual Aramaic
speech of the Chaldeans. It is still more surprising to notice
that after having once used this language, he continues in
it all the way to the conclusion of chapter 7, at which place
he reverts once more to Hebrew. Why then is about half
the book written in Aramaic and the other half in Hebrew?
First, "it should be carefully observed that in the Babylon
of the late sixth century, in which Daniel purportedly lived,
the predominant language spoken by the heterogeneous
population of this metropolis was Aramaic. It is therefore
not surprising that an inhabitant of that city should have
resorted to Aramaic in composing a portion of his mem-
oirs."[6]

Daniel does not in so many words give his reasons for
writing one particular portion in Hebrew and the other in
Aramaic, but the hypothesis has been suggested, which
seems reasonable, that what especially pertained to Israel
and was for the comfort and edification of God's ancient
people was written in Hebrew, whereas chapters 2-7, being
more general in nature, were made easily available to the
people among whom the prophet lived.

Hebrew was the language of Daniel's people, the language in which the oracles of God were made known to

[5]Gleason L. Archer, Jr., *A Survey of Old Testament Introduction*, p. 12.
[6]Archer, p. 378.

the covenant people, Israel. . . . Chapter one and chapters eight through twelve are in Hebrew, appropriate for a message concerning and addressed to the Hebrew people. . . . Chapters two through seven are written in Aramaic. Aramaic was not at the time of Daniel the language of Israel. We now know that it was then, had been for some time, and continued to be for several centuries, the lingua franca of the ancient world. What koine Greek was to the nations of earth during the Greek age, what Latin has been among most of the nations of the Western world up to modern times, what French is to international diplomacy now, Aramaic was to the Neo-Babylonian Empire . . . [and was] appropriate for a message concerning Gentile people and kings, and though addressed to God's people, is instructive also for those same Gentile peoples and kings.[7]

To return to the Chaldeans—their amazement at the king's command can easily be imagined. To be required to recount the dream itself without having previously heard it was something they had little anticipated. It may be that Nebuchadnezzar was already suspicious of their supposed knowledge from past experience, for he accused them of stalling, so to speak. He felt that they were trying to put him off with evasive words "till the time be changed." By this expression he possibly meant that they were trying to delay matters until enough time had passed for his anger to cool, so that he might rescind his sentence upon them. Or it may even be that he actually suspected them of plotting treason against him, and of seeking to evade him until such time as a new ruler might sit upon the throne.

"You are trying to gain time," said Nebuchadnezzar. The word translated "gain" is literally "buy." Because of the

[7]Robert D. Culver, *Daniel and the Latter Days*, p. 98.

evil of the present moment, they were trying to buy all the time they could until a more favorable day might come. This reminds us forcibly of Ephesians 5:16 where Christians are urged to "redeem" (buy up) the time "because the days are evil." As these men sought to buy up time for themselves because of the evil moments in which they were living, so we are to buy up time—not for ourselves, but for God, in view of the evil days in which we are living. Every moment must count for Christ and His cause.

The answer the Chaldeans gave to the king was rather pathetic. Their complaint that no other monarch had ever made such a requirement may doubtless have been true, but would mean little to Nebuchadnezzar who was quite used to making such demands. The statement that only the gods "whose dwelling is not with flesh" could reveal such a secret is somehow touching. Ignorant idolaters as they were, these men knew enough to confess that there are great riddles in the universe which can be revealed only by supernatural powers, and they themselves were unable to contact such powers. Thank God for the grand reply of John 1:14: "And the Word was made flesh, and dwelt among us, (and we beheld his glory, the glory as of the only begotten of the Father) full of grace and truth." What a great verity the Samaritan woman spoke when she said: "I know that Messias cometh, which is called Christ: when he is come, he will tell us all things" (John 4:25). In Christ the living Word, God incarnate dwells among men and reveals to them His divine secrets (Col. 2:3).

On hearing the Chaldeans acknowledge their inability to reconstruct the dream, the king fell into a terrible rage. In his anger he ordered the early execution of all the wise men

in his realm. At this point Daniel and his three friends
came into the story, since they were now numbered among
Babylon's wise men.

THE INTERPRETER FOUND (2:14-30)

Daniel and his companions had clearly not been present
when the wise men were interviewed by Nebuchadnezzar.
But when the king's captain came around to gather them
for execution, Daniel inquired as to why such a command
had been given in so hasty a manner, when not all the wise
men had as yet been consulted. The details, previously
unknown to him, were explained by Arioch.

Immediately on learning the complete story, Daniel
asked of the king additional time in order to discover the
interpretation. A later verse (v. 25) makes it clear that
Daniel at this time did not see the king in person, but evidently through the mediation of some courtier obtained a
brief respite. It seems that God was at work again, since
Daniel secured what the magicians could not. Of course,
there was a difference in the request he made. The magicians asked for the *dream;* Daniel promised to give the
dream but asked only for *time.* This request was granted
him by the king.

His next act was not to go to the library to consult books
on the interpretation of dreams. He did not even go to his
friends for advice. Instead he called them to a prayer meeting. It is good to have praying friends! Those who walk
closest to God still realize their need of much intercession.
Paul constantly requested prayer for himself and his ministry (Rom. 15:30; I Cor. 1:11; Eph. 6:18-19; Phil. 1:19;
Col. 4:2-3; I Thess. 5:25; II Thess. 3:1; Philemon 22) .

It is important to notice that these men were already on

"praying ground." When trials cause thoughtless men and women to turn to God, there is cause for rejoicing. But it is far better to be walking in fellowship with the Lord before the trials come.

The title Daniel used of God (vv. 18-19) is of special interest—"the God of heaven." With Israel dispersed because of disobedience, God is no longer called "the God of Israel," the God who dwells among His people on earth, but instead "the God of heaven." This expression is found only in the books of Nehemiah, Ezekiel, Daniel and Revelation.

The answer to the prayer meeting was not long in coming. God gave the answer and Daniel gave thanks. God's children often forget to praise Him when He graciously answers their prayers. Daniel did not forget to say thank you to God. This little sequence is said by Ironside to reveal the process of true worship: first comes prayer (v. 18), then divine ministry, then worship (v. 19):

> People have very low ideas about worship nowadays; they talk about worshiping God no matter what religious exercise they may be engaged in. But let us remember that even prayer is not worship, and ministry is not worship. Prayer is asking of God; ministry is when God gives something to man. But when man has asked, and God has given till the heart is full and it overflows in adoration back to God, this is worship.[8]

Daniel in his grateful response spoke beautifully of God's almighty wisdom, His omniscience, His omnipotence. If, as a captive in a strange land, Daniel could see God's hand in control, how can we ever doubt this fact? God "changes times and seasons"—the very prophecy soon to be

[8]Ironside, p. 31.

given in this chapter reveals the accuracy of this statement. Another illustration: Many years later the rulers in the time of Christ determined not to kill Him during the Passover season lest the people be aroused (Matt. 26:3-5). But God decreed otherwise, and so the "times and seasons" set by men were changed, and our Lord, the "Lamb of God," was slain during the very feast that so aptly typified His death (John 18:39).

God controls the rise and fall of this earth's rulers; it is He who gives ability to the wise and prudent (v. 21). He is not only a God who knows all things, but He reveals His wonderful plans and purposes to His children who, like these four young men, are in intimate relationship with Himself (v. 22). Nothing is hidden from His all-seeing eye. Daniel acknowledged that all his own power and wisdom were gifts of God (v. 23). He also thanked God for the special answer to prayer granted them, even before he faced Nebuchadnezzar.

Now he was ready to see the king. Arioch brought him into Nebuchadnezzar's presence, and tried to claim a bit of merit for himself in bringing to the king what he felt would be pleasing news (v. 25). This might be expected from a worldly courtier. But how different was the attitude of Daniel! He claimed nothing for himself but instead gave all the glory to God (v. 30).

In his opening words to the king, Daniel made it clear that the dream was a prophetic one (v. 27). God was revealing to Nebuchadnezzar what was to be "in the latter days." From the vantage point of the day in which we now live, we can see that much of the dream has already been fulfilled, but that a part still remains to be accomplished in the yet future.

Before Nebuchadnezzar, Daniel disclaimed emphatically the possession of any special wisdom of his own. The men most used of God have always been those who sought no glory of their own but ascribed all the praise and honor to Him. The expression "for their sakes that shall make known the interpretation" (v. 30) is an Aramaic idiom meaning "to the intent that the interpretation may be made known the the king."[9] When Daniel said that the dream was given "that thou mightest know the thoughts of thy heart," he meant that Nebuchadnezzar was now to have the answer to those thoughts he had in mind before falling asleep and having this unusual dream. Daniel certainly confirmed Nebuchadnezzar's opinion that the dream was by no means an ordinary one.

The question sometimes arises as to whether God speaks to people in dreams today. Undoubtedly He *can* and it may be that sometimes He *does,* but if so, it happens very seldom. Possessing now His complete revelation we no longer need dreams and visions. "God, who at sundry times and in divers manners spake in time past unto the fathers by the prophets, hath in these last days spoken unto us by his Son" (Heb. 1:1-2).

THE DREAM AND ITS INTERPRETATION GIVEN
(2:31-45)

In brief words Daniel sketched first the king's dream and then its meaning. In his vision Nebuchadnezzar saw a great majestic image of a man standing upright. This image represented the various Gentile world powers. In chapter 7 when God showed His servant Daniel a picture of similar scope the imagery changed to ravenous beasts.

[9]Jamieson, Fausset and Brown, IV, 390.

Nebuchadnezzar saw the imposing outward power and splendour of 'the times of the Gentiles' . . . while Daniel saw the true character of Gentile world-government as rapacious and warlike, established and maintained by force. It is remarkable that the heraldic insignia of the Gentile nations are all beasts or birds of prey.[10]

The expression "a great image" is in the original language literally "one image that was great."[11] Though this image was composed of different metals nevertheless it was one. Likewise the kingdoms it represented, though different, form essentially one world power during the "times of the Gentiles," and that power is inspired by the "god of this world" (II Cor. 4:4). The image was said to be both excellent and terrible. This world power is excellent to those who profit by it, but terrible to those—and they are many—who suffer oppression at its hand.

The mighty statue had a head of fine gold, breast and arms of silver, belly and thighs of brass, legs of iron, and feet of iron and clay mixed. As Nebuchadnezzar viewed it in amazement, suddenly and without warning a "stone cut out without hands" smote the colossus and completely demolished it. The stone then became a great mountain filling the whole earth.

After this description Daniel did not say, "Is this the dream?" but rather, "This is the dream." He knew that God had spoken revealing this secret to him. Nebuchadnezzar doubtless silently nodded, by his very speechlessness consenting to the accuracy of Daniel's reconstruction of the vision.

Daniel then went on to the interpretation: The head of

[10]C. I. Scofield, Scofield Reference Bible, pp. 910-11, n.d.
[11]Jamieson, Fausset and Brown, *ibid.*

gold represented Nebuchadnezzar himself and his kingdom
of Babylon. He had been made by God a universal ruler.
This does not mean that he actually reigned over the entire globe. But he could have. All was "given into his
hand" and he could have appropriated any part of it at will.
"Universal dominion" was never fully realized but power
was given for it.[12] Even though Nebuchadnezzar at this
time did not know the true God nor serve Him, yet He
was the One who had given him all the blessings he possessed. This is likewise true of us today. Every blessing
we enjoy, whether we realize it or not, is from God. "Every
good gift and every perfect gift is from above, and cometh
down from the Father of lights" (James 1:17).

The kingdom to follow Babylon is represented by the
silver breast and arms. This world empire is stated in
Daniel 5:28 to be Media-Persia. It is said by Daniel to be
inferior to Nebuchadnezzar's kingdom. Although Prideaux
affirms that "the kings of Persia were the worst race of men
that ever governed an empire,"[13] it seems more likely that
the term referred to the power of the rulers rather than to
the quality of their character. Nebuchadnezzar's word was
absolute law (Dan. 5:18-19). The record in Daniel 6 makes
it clear that the kings of Media-Persia however were not
absolute monarchs, but were themselves subject to the law.

The kingdom which was to succeed Media-Persia was
described as "another third kingdom of brass, which shall
bear rule over all the earth." This empire is identified by
name in Daniel 8:21 as Greece. History tells us that Alexander the Great actually commanded that he be called
"king of all the world."[14] The two thighs in the image may

[12]Scofield, p. 901, margin.
[13]Jamieson, Fausset and Brown, IV, 392.
[14]*Ibid.*

speak of the fact that this empire was, like Media-Persia, a combination of two adjacent countries—Greece and Macedonia.

The iron legs represented a fourth great world empire, which was to arise following that of Greece. This fourth kingdom is not named in the Old Testament, but immediately one opens the New he reads: "And it came to pass in those days, that there went out a decree from Caesar Augustus, that all the world should be taxed" (Luke 2:1). This testifies that the prophecy of Daniel found its fulfillment in the great Roman Empire. Iron well typifies the resistless power of that kingdom.

Between verses 40 and 41 there is an unreckoned period of time. The legs of iron spoke of the commencement of the Roman Empire. But the vision then passed abruptly to the final state of that kingdom, at a time just prior to the second coming of the Lord Jesus Christ. This period was symbolized by the feet and toes which were part of iron and part of clay. Thus between these two verses is to be found what has sometimes been called "the great parenthesis" of Old Testament prophecy.[15] We now know that between the rise of the Roman Empire and its reconstruction in the last days of this age, something previously unannounced in the program of God has appeared—the present dispensation of grace. The present church age and its length were not revealed to Daniel nor to the other prophets of the Old Testament period.

Thus the final picture in the prophecy yet remains to be fulfilled. At some later but unspecified time the condition is to develop represented by the feet and toes "part of potters' clay and part of iron." This mixture Ironside in-

---

[15]See Ironside, *The Great Parenthesis.*

terprets as "an attempted union between imperialism and democracy."[16] By comparison with Daniel 7:24 and Revelation 17:12-13, the ten toes can with confidence be said to represent ten kings (or dictators) who will reign in the last days, but who will form a confederacy in the territory once controlled by the Roman Empire, for there is to be a continuation of the Roman iron, even though in an adulterated state. This confederacy of the last days could well be called "the reconstituted Roman Empire." On this yet future period, the later prophecies of Daniel cast considerable additional light.

The most striking feature of Nebuchadnezzar's dream, however, was the demolishing of the great image by the stone "cut out of the mountain without hands." Daniel carefully explained that during the days of the ten kings (symbolized by the ten toes) God shall set up His kingdom of glory on earth. The stone speaks of Christ at His second advent (*i.e.,* of Christ as the stone).[17] Other prophecies using a like symbolism may be found in such texts as Psalm 118:22; Isaiah 8:14; 28:16; Zechariah 3:9; Acts 4:11; I Peter 2:7-8.

THE AFTERMATH (2:46-49)

Nebuchadnezzar was so affected by Daniel's supernatural knowledge that he worshiped Daniel, thereby acknowledging that God had truly spoken through him. Although it is not recorded here, Daniel doubtless rejected such wor-

---

[16]Ironside, *Lectures on Daniel* . . . , pp. 36-37.
[17]It has been suggested that this might refer to the first coming of Christ. However it is quite obvious that Gentile world power was not by any means destroyed at that time. In fact the Roman Empire continued on hundreds of years longer. Also the condition of ten kings reigning did not exist when Christ came the first time, and indeed *could not* exist until the iron Roman Empire was dissolved and reconstituted.

ship, as God's true servants have always done (Acts 10:25-
26), and rather gave the glory to God. Nebuchadnezzar's
words in verse 47 appear to be an answer to some such statement on the part of Daniel. His expression was excellent
so far as it went, but obviously it did not go far enough.
He still saw God as only one among others—the greatest of
the gods. However he highly honored Daniel, and at the
latter's request the three faithful friends were not forgotten.

3

THE FAITHFUL JEWS IN THE FIERY FURNACE

(3:1-30)

NEBUCHADNEZZAR'S IMAGE WORSHIP (3:1-7)

THE FIRST QUESTION of interest that arises as one begins this chapter is in regard to the time when this striking scene took place. Fausset states that nineteen years elapsed between chapters 2 and 3;[1] Matthew Henry suggests seven years.[2] As there is no direct statement in the text, any such figure must of necessity be speculation. Does not the story itself seem to indicate that a very short time passed between these two chapters? The dream of the great image was still quite fresh in the mind of Nebuchadnezzar. He actually constructed a similar image but different in one most significant way from that of the vision. In the divinely revealed image only the head was of gold; all of Nebuchadnezzar's was of this metal. The head of gold represented Nebuchadnezzar (2:38). At the time the dream was interpreted, the Babylonian king, stunned by the greatness of the revelation, had been apparently content with this position assigned

[1]Jamieson, Fausset and Brown, *Commentary*, IV, 396.
[2]Matthew Henry, *Commentary on the Whole Bible*, p. 1034.

him. But later his overweening pride reasserted itself and
he wanted to be not just the head but the whole. So his
own image he made *all* of gold. For a time he had been
deeply convicted but "strong convictions often come short
of a sound conversion."[3] He did not yet know Jehovah as
other than one among many gods (Dan. 2:47).

The gigantic image he constructed was 60 by 6 cubits—
approximately 90 by 9 feet in our measurements.[4] The
nine-foot breadth probably refers to the distance through
the chest to the back; this would make a well-proportioned
figure. As to whether the statue and base totaled ninety
feet in height, or the image alone measured that distance
is immaterial. Regardless of the exact construction, it was
clearly a monumental figure. Judging by the immense size,
the image probably was overlaid with gold, rather than
being solidly constructed of that precious metal; but even
so it must have been a splendid sight to behold, set up in
the Plain of Dura. This plain was evidently quite close to
the city, possibly within the very walls of Babylon, but its
exact site is now unknown.

The fact that two 6's are used in the dimensions of this
figure reminds the Bible reader forcibly of Revelation
13:13-18. In those verses the number of the Antichrist, the
beast-king of the last days, is said to be 666. Without attempting any sensational interpretation, it may be safely
said that 6 is the number of man, the number of incomple-
tion and imperfection, just as 7 is the number of God, the
divine, the perfect, the complete number.[5] So three 6's, to

[3]Henry, p. 1035.
[4]The cubit was "an important and constant measure among the Hebrews and other ancient nations. It was commonly reckoned as the length
of the arm from the point of the elbow to the end of the middle finger,
about 18 inches" (Merrill F. Unger, *Unger's Bible Dictionary*, p. 720).
[5]S. Edwin Hartill, *Biblical Hermeneutics*, pp. 114-15.

say the least, represent the very highest peak man is able to attain, but yet a height that is far below the perfection and almighty power of God. The fact that two 6's are mentioned in connection with Nebuchadnezzar's image suggests that this scene in some measure foreshadows the setting up of the Antichrist's image in the temple at Jerusalem during the last days of this age. This is what Daniel (and the Lord Jesus Christ) referred to as "the abomination of desolation." More is said about this in the later studies of the present volume.

For the dedication of his image, Nebuchadnezzar summoned all the officials of the land, both civil and military, who together with the nobility were commanded to be present. If all these obeyed the king, there was no doubt that the common people would do likewise. When the day arrived and the assemblage was complete, the king's herald gave a command. First there was to be the playing of an orchestra—with sensual music the emotions of the people were to be aroused. Then at a given signal, all were to bow down and worship the golden image, on penalty of being thrown into a fiery furnace. Thus means were used both to allure and frighten the people into this idolatrous act. In Satan's dealings with us today, he still uses one or both of these methods to try to get us to do that which is displeasing to God. He seeks to make the way of sin seem very enticing and the way of righteousness very repelling.

THE FAITHFUL JEWS ACCUSED (3:8-12)

Actually the only people vitally affected by the king's order were the Jews. The idol-worshiping Gentiles were not required to cease worshiping their own gods, but only to make the addition of one more image. It is at first sur-

prising to observe that the accusation against the three
Hebrew youths was made by the Chaldeans—the very people who had previously been condemned to death for their
inability to tell the king's dream, and whose lives had been
saved by the prayer meeting of these three youths and their
friend Daniel. How could these Chaldeans have been
guilty of such base ingratitude? Alas, ingratitude is a sad
attribute of fallen human nature. Probably these men
were jealous of Daniel and his friends because of their
elevation to high office and rewards which they had originally hoped to secure for themselves. In some ways jealousy is the most terrible of all the passions (Prov. 6:34;
Song of Sol. 8:6). A tremendous amount of the world's
injustice and confusion is the result of jealousy. Sad to
say it is found all too often even among Christians. In
many churches the work of Christ is hindered because of
jealousy among the members of the body of Christ. "My
brethren, these things ought not so to be."

The malicious Chaldeans began their speech to the king
with flattery, before reminding him of his cruel order and
finally accusing Hananiah, Mishael and Azariah. They im-
plied that the young Jews were ungrateful, that they had
obstinately refused to obey King Nebuchadnezzar, even
though he had been exceedingly kind to them, and had
set them, foreigners though they were, "over the affairs of
the province of Babylon." They further claimed that the
three did not have proper respect for the king: "These
men, O king, have not regarded thee." This was utterly
false. They did respect the king, and had obeyed his command so far as conscience would permit them. They had
not failed to present themselves at the required place, but
once there they would not even for Nebuchadnezzar him-

self break the second commandment. Truly these boys knew the meaning of Peter's great words: "We ought to obey God rather than men" (Acts 5:29). It is obvious from the conversation of the Chaldeans with the king that Nebuchadnezzar had not given his order especially to trap the young Jews. If so he would have been watching them to see how they would respond. However the conduct of the Chaldeans leads to the surmise that they may have instigated the king to his entire action, even as men of a similar stamp later instigated Darius to sign his foolish decree (Dan. 6:6-9).

Readers of this chapter have often asked, "Where was Daniel?" Of course no human being can give a definite answer to this question, since our entire information on the subject is found in the Bible, and the Bible gives no hint as to Daniel's whereabouts on this occasion. If speculation must be indulged in, there seem to be three possible explanations: (1) Daniel was away at some distant point of the realm engaged in official business. (2) Daniel was in Babylon, but was not required to be present and bow to the image. This may well be the true answer, as it seems from 2:46 that the king felt that Daniel ought himself to be worshiped, and may therefore not have required one he felt to be a superior being to worship the image. (3) Daniel was present, and took the same stand as his three friends, but the Chaldeans were afraid to accuse him, knowing of Nebuchadnezzar's high regard for and awe of the young prophet. One thing may be said with certainty—if Daniel was present, he did not bow down to the image, for he always had the courage of his convictions.

As a matter of fact, the omission of any reference to Daniel in this chapter is in itself an excellent argument for the historicity of the book. If the writer had merely been concocting an imaginative story of fiction (as some modern critics claim), is it possible that in this chapter, which contains perhaps the most striking scene in the entire book, the author would have left out completely his principal character? Absolutely not! If this book were fiction, Daniel would have been represented as leading the three youths in their bold stand. But since it records fact, the author does not even seek to explain the absence of Daniel, since the reason for it was likely known to the original readers already.

THE FAITHFUL JEWS REFUSE TO WORSHIP THE IMAGE (3:13-18)

Although angry at their disobedience, the king still had enough regard for the young men to question them personally. He did not order their immediate destruction, but instead offered them another chance. His word to them was simply "turn or burn." Rashly forgetting the admission he had made in Daniel 2:47, he defied God Himself: "Who is that God that shall deliver you out of my hands?"

Confronted by a wrathful king, the young men steadfastly refused to worship the image. Matthew Henry suggests seven reasons that these three youths might have used in persuading themselves that they should comply with the king's command.[6] In somewhat adapted form, they are:

1. They were not required to turn from the worship of the true God, nor to make any profession as to this image, but only to bow to it.

2. They were not required to adopt idolatry, but only to commit one act which they might later have declared

---

[6]Henry, p. 1039.

their sorrow for, and sought forgiveness from God. Surely I John 1:9 was as true then as now!

3. The king, who commanded this act, had absolute power and they were forced to do his will. Therefore the responsibility for any evil would be his alone. War criminals at the close of World War II offered just such an excuse at the Nuremberg Trials.[7]

4. Nebuchadnezzar had been their benefactor, had educated and honored them. It would seem right to strain their consciences a bit to show their gratitude to him.

5. They were in a strange land, and so might easily have been excused for following the customs of that country. "When in Rome do as the Romans do."

6. Their ancestors—even the kings, princes and priests—had often worshiped idols, even on occasion setting them up in the very temple of God. Their own act would be much less grievous.

7. By complying with the king's decree, they would save their lives, keep their high positions, and thus be able to help the people of God in their hour of great need. On the other hand, if they refused the king, their lives would be snuffed out in a moment and would be of value to no one. This is simply the old argument that the end justifies the means. The Scripture frequently informs us that such a principle is never valid (see Rom. 3:8).

With seven excuses such as these, Daniel's friends might easily have sought to justify themselves for bowing down to the king's image. On the other hand, only one reason could be found for refusing to bow. But that one is worth more than the seven combined—the direct command of God in Exodus 20:4-6:

[7]Joseph L. Morse (ed.), *The Universal Standard Encyclopaedia*, XVII, 6241.

Thou shalt not make unto thee any graven image, or any likeness of any thing that is in heaven above, or that is in the earth beneath, or that is in the water under the earth. Thou shalt not bow down thyself to them, nor serve them: for I the LORD thy God am a jealous God, visiting the iniquity of the fathers upon the children unto the third and fourth generation of them that hate me; and shewing mercy unto thousands of them that love me, and keep my commandments.

The noble reply the youths actually made to the king is deserving of much study and meditation. Unlike the Chaldeans, they affirmed that they would give the king a clear answer and attempt no evasion. They expressed their confidence in the fact that God was able to deliver them from the fiery furnace if He wished. Since Nebuchadnezzar had cast out a challenge to God, they rather felt that God would answer it and deliver them. But the grandest words in their entire speech are those three little ones "but if not." Regardless of temporal deliverance they would not disobey God. May such ever be our own attitude! When trials come, we know that God is able to deliver us, if He chooses. But even if He does not choose to do so, let us be determined to still remain firm, reposing our confidence in Him. Romans 8:28 is an eternal truth: "And we know that all things work together for good to them that love God, to them who are the called according to his purpose." The trials when God does not seem to hear are the ones that truly test faith. These boys wonderfully stood the test.

THE FAITHFUL JEWS CAST INTO THE FIERY FURNACE
(3:19-23)

The courageous answer of the young men terribly enraged Nebuchadnezzar. His face contorted with anger, he commanded that the furnace be heated seven times more than usual. Without any respite, clothed as they were, Hananiah, Mishael and Azariah were cast into the fearful furnace.

What an awful death! But if such a fate seems horrible, remember it is not to be compared with the second death in the lake of fire, which the Bible says will be the future punishment of sinners without a Saviour (Rev. 20:15). Jesus Christ, speaking of the Nebuchadnezzars of this world, said: "Be not afraid of them that kill the body, and after that have no more that they can do. But I will forewarn you whom ye shall fear: Fear him, which after he hath killed hath power to cast into hell; yea, I say unto you, Fear him" (Luke 12:4-5).

The fire was so hot that it blasted the men who carried the three youths to cast them into the furnace, and these soldiers were no weaklings but the mightiest men in the entire army. Judgment fell swiftly on these servants of the king. While it is true that they were obeying his orders, doubtless they found sadistic pleasure in their role. But they were destroyed. As for Nebuchadnezzar, he was to be dealt with later by a holy and righteous God. One Bible expositor has well written: "There is a day coming when proud tyrants will be punished, not only for the cruelties they have been guilty of, but for employing those about them in their cruelties, and so exposing them to the judgments of God."[8] Notice, by the way, it is said that the three youths "fell down" into the furnace, from which it is evident that they were in some manner cast in from above.

[8]Henry, p. 1040.

The Faithful Jews Delivered and Honored
(3:24-30)

It appears that the king had some sort of peephole by which he alone could view the interior of the furnace. As he made his observation in this manner, astonishment suddenly passed over his face, and he hurriedly inquired as to the number of men cast into the furnace. When assured that there were but three, he revealed the fact that he saw a fourth Person walking in the flames, and this One he declared to be "like the Son of God." Evidently he did not fully understand the meaning of his words, for in verse 28 he called this Person "an angel." But in his ignorance he spoke a remarkable truth. This glorious Person could have been no other than the preincarnate Christ, appearing to fulfill the promise made in Isaiah 43:1-2: "But now thus saith the LORD that created thee, O Jacob, and he that formed thee, O Israel, Fear not: for I have redeemed thee, I have called thee by thy name; thou art mine. When thou passest through the waters, I will be with thee; and through the rivers, they shall not overflow thee: when thou walkest through the fire, thou shalt not be burned; neither shall the flame kindle upon thee."

Nebuchadnezzar soon saw that only one thing about these young men had been consumed by the fire—the ropes with which they were bound, for now they were "loose." Convinced by this great miracle that he did wrong in attempting to destroy the three Hebrews, the king personally called them forth. He acknowledged that Jehovah their Lord was the Most High God, and that these young men had a loftier allegiance than to himself—they were "servants of the most High God." This indeed is truly a "high calling" (Phil. 3:14).

The Babylonians were not credulous savages, willing to accept anything a bit out of the ordinary as a miracle. The record states that a most careful examination was made of these three Hebrew young men after they came forth from the furnace. This "scientific investigation" revealed that their bodies had not been burned, their hair had not been singed, their coats had not been scorched, and most amazing of all, not even the *smell* of smoke was about their persons.

Then Nebuchadnezzar acknowledged that Hananiah, Mishael and Azariah were right in obeying their God, even if it meant disobeying him. When one stands true for God, eventually even his opponents will be brought to respect him. The king decreed that no one should speak anything against the God of these youths. Before the miracle Nebuchadnezzar had asked: "Who is that God that shall deliver you out of my hands?" He found the answer to his question, for after the miracle he exclaimed: "There is no other God that can deliver after this sort."

The concluding verse of the chapter records the satisfying fact that the three young men in the end had even greater honor bestowed on them than before: "Then the king promoted Shadrach, Meshach, and Abed-nego, in the province of Babylon."

4

THE HUMBLING OF NEBUCHADNEZZAR

(4:1-37)

THIS PASSAGE IS UNIQUE in the Bible in that the entire chapter consists of a proclamation or edict written by King Nebuchadnezzar and incorporated for obvious reasons into Daniel's book. The incident is a graphic illustration of Job 33:14-17. God spoke to Nebuchadnezzar once in the dream recorded in chapter 2. Again He spoke in the miracle of the fiery furnace. But Nebuchadnezzar, in his pride and arrogance, continued in his willful way until God spoke this third time. Even then he did not heed the Lord's voice until he was utterly humbled. God made this man the great king of all the earth, but that did not satisfy him. He sought after divine honors and placed his will against that of God. Then the same God who gave him his greatness took it away, and brought him as low as the beasts of the field.

The words with which the chapter opens are revealing. They are from the heart of the king after God had dealt

with him. His former arrogance is missing and a new
spirit of humility is manifested. Doubtless all of his sub-
jects had known something of his unusual experience, but
he thought it fitting that a testimony should come directly
from his own lips. Testimony for God is good—when it
brings glory to Him. Nebuchadnezzar speaks of the "wonders" God had wrought toward him—the reference being to
the dream, the interpretation and the resulting fulfillment.
As a result of this experience he came to realize in a whole-
some way the shortness of his own dominion and the
eternity of God's.

NEBUCHADNEZZAR'S DREAM OF THE GREAT TREE
(4:4-18)

At the time this episode in his life began, the king was
in an apparently secure position—all enemies conquered
and not a cloud on the horizon. No human hand dared
to rise against him. But remember God can deal with un-
godly men when human resistance cannot, even when all
seems well with them. The wicked may sometimes possess
a false security and imagine all to be well even on the very
brink of their doom.

At this point in his career another miraculous dream
was granted to Nebuchadnezzar, many years after the one
of chapter 2. This time he did not forget the dream. Indeed he vividly remembered it with terrifying thoughts,
and he certainly was not a man to be easily frightened.
Although he knew Daniel and his ability yet he turned
first to the Chaldeans, and again found them powerless.
Even today it is sometimes true that those who know the
Lord and have received blessed answers to prayer in the
past, when a new problem arises, will turn to various

human expedients before seeking the Lord's face! The
Chaldeans, false prophets that they were, though they had
previously claimed ability to interpret a dream once they
were told it, failed even in this boast.

When the others had failed, Daniel was finally summoned. Men whose hearts are not right with God usually
dislike to face His messengers. So Daniel was called only
as a last resort. Nebuchadnezzar still spoke to him as a
heathen polytheist, talking of many "gods," but he used the
term "holy," which was applied only to Jehovah. Daniel
was acknowledged "master of magicians," the man who
succeeded when the magicians failed. Nebuchadnezzar was
sure about Daniel that "no secret troubleth thee"—nothing
was too difficult for his interpretation.

A description of the prophetic dream was then given to
Daniel. The central feature was a great tree, located in the
most conspicuous place on earth. This tree grew and increased until it reached to heaven and could be seen by all
the earth. It was pleasant to look upon and its fruit was
good to eat. Not only did it provide beauty and nourish-
ment, but also protection to the beasts of the field in its
shadow, and to the birds of the air in its branches. But as
the king marveled, suddenly and unexpectedly there came
an order for the destruction of this apparently indestructi-
ble tree. Although no human woodsman could accomplish
such a task "a watcher and an holy one came down from
heaven" with God's decree of judgment. This "watcher"
was doubtless a holy angel. These beings behold the deeds
of men, and are "ministering spirits" to the saints of God
(Heb. 1:14).

The decree proclaimed that the great tree was to be cut
down, the branches removed, the leaves shaken from the

branches, the fruit scattered, the beasts lodging under it and the fowls lodging in it driven away. The picture was one of almost complete destruction. But even in God's wrath there was mercy. The stump and the roots were to be left in the earth: it was not to be uprooted. This stump was then to be subject to all the elements and to the beasts of the field.

The angel in part interpreted the vision; he eventually spoke no longer of the tree as it, but as he (vv. 15-16). Clearly the tree represented a person who was to have his heart changed from a man's to a beast's. "The heart in Scripture is variously used, sometimes for the mind and understanding, sometimes for the will, sometimes for the affections, sometimes for the conscience, sometimes for the whole soul. Generally, it denotes the whole soul of man and all the faculties of it."[1] In this dream it evidently referred primarily to the reason (for similar usages, see Gen. 8:21; Deut. 8:5; Isa. 44:19). The person represented in the dream was to have his human intellect made like a beast's, and that for a period of seven years.

Verse 17 refers again, this time in the plural, to "watchers" and "holy ones." In solemn assembly the holy angels had not only subscribed to God's righteous decree in this matter, but had made it their demand. The angels evidently demand judgment on any mortal who seeks to take God's glory from Him.

All is done "that the living may know that the most High ruleth in the kingdom of men." Like others in high position, Nebuchadnezzar had ignored the fact that all his prosperity was due to the blessing of the Almighty. He needed to be forcibly reminded that God is sovereign in

[1]James Orr (ed.), *International Standard Bible Encyclopaedia*, II, 1351.

His control. To demonstrate this, He sometimes "setteth up over it the basest of men" and accomplishes His purposes even through them.

When he had related the dream, the king expressed confidence that Daniel would be able to interpret it, and then waited for the prophet to speak.

THE DREAM INTERPRETED BY DANIEL (4:19-27)

Evidently the interpretation of the dream was from the beginning clear to Daniel. But stunned by the magnitude of the judgment about to befall the king, Daniel stood speechless for one whole hour. Despite his faults, Nebuchadnezzar had been kind to Daniel, and the latter had a high regard for him. For this reason he "was astonied [was stricken dumb, ASV] for one hour."[2] Seeing that Daniel was troubled, the king encouraged him to go on, indicating that he was ready to receive whatever the prophet had to tell him. Daniel, after courteously indicating that he would prefer to see such a judgment fall upon the king's enemies rather than upon Nebuchadnezzar himself, proceeded fearlessly to proclaim God's Word.

The tree represented Nebuchadnezzar himself. With this key the individual details were clear enough and needed little interpretation. The most significant feature of the dream was the felling of the tree. Daniel interpreted this as meaning that Nebuchadnezzar was to be driven from his throne and made to dwell among the beasts for seven years: "Till thou know that the most High ruleth in the kingdom of men, and giveth it to whomsoever he

---

[2]"It is to be noted here that the word *sha'a*, translated 'hour,' has no such definite meaning; Gesenius gives, 'a moment of time,' in which he is followed by Bevan, Keil, and Stuart" (*Pulpit Commentary*, XIII, 140). The ASV renders the expression "for a while."

will." Nebuchadnezzar, in his pride and presumption, had
come to imagine that his own strength and ability had obtained for him his high position. He had to be humbled
until he was willing to confess that he was nothing and
God was all. Even today God cannot and will not use any
person to the fullest until he is ready to make this same
confession.

The final item of interpretation was the promise that
after the king was willing to "humble himself under the
mighty hand of God," in due time he would be exalted
again (I Peter 5:6). However, Daniel did not close without a faithful word of exhortation, advising him to repent
and turn from his sins. If so, it was suggested as a possi-
bility ("it may be") that God would lengthen his tran-
quillity. Just how the Lord would do this the prophet did
not undertake to explain, but he doubtless meant either
by prolonging the time before the judgment or shortening
it when it did come. It seems that Daniel had no direct
word from God on this phase of the matter, but he was able
to make such a suggestion because of his knowledge that
God is a God of love and is always ready to show mercy
to those who turn to Him (cf. Jonah 4:2).

THE DREAM FULFILLED AND ITS RESULT (4:28-37)

Sad to say, Nebuchadnezzar even after this warning did
not repent nor turn from his evil way. Nevertheless, in
His grace, God gave an additional year of respite. Then
came a climactic moment when Nebuchadnezzar, survey-
ing the wonders of the city of Babylon, became inflated
with pride and directly challenged God by ascribing the
glory to himself: "Is not this great Babylon, that I have

built?"[3] While the boastful word was in his very mouth,
leaving no doubt as to the cause of the judgment, immediately the king was smitten. The tragic result of his vain-
glory was that he who had attempted to make himself more
than a man became less than human. His kingdom, seemingly so secure, was in an instant gone from him, along
with his reason as well. Of course there were no mental

[3]It should not be thought that Nebuchadnezzar was foolishly magnifying some insignificant shantytown into a fine city. Humanly speaking he
was well warranted in considering his capital "great Babylon." The following description is derived from *Archaeology and the Bible*, G. Frederick Owen, pp. 121-24, and Fairbairn, *Imperial Standard Bible Encyclopaedia*, I, 243-45, who calls it "the largest and most powerful city of
antiquity." The city was a square, 15 miles in length on each side. There
were wide streets, strong fortifications and numerous public buildings.
There was still sufficient land left for farming and pasture to supply the
needs of all the inhabitants. The population was apparently about
1,200,000. The city was surrounded by a deep, wide moat, filled with
water, next to which was a wall 87 feet broad and 350 feet high. The top
of the wall was wide enough for four chariots to be driven abreast. There
were streets intersecting the city and running to the twelve gates. The
river Euphrates ran through the city but there were tall levees on either
side to prevent it from damaging things when it was at flood stage. In
addition there were canals to carry excess water to the Tigris River.
According to Strabo, Babylon contained two of the seven wonders of the
ancient world: the high wall and the "hanging gardens." The gardens
were built by Nebuchadnezzar to please his wife Amytis who wearied
of the level country and pined for the wooded hills of her native land,
Media. Actually the "hanging gardens" were a man-made hill, 400 feet in
length on each side and rising to a height of 350 feet. Amytis was able
to climb to the top by means of a ten-foot-wide staircase. There was
terrace after terrace, each supported by vaultings which were hollow and
contained enough earth to permit the growth of the largest trees. Though
the structure was made of baked bricks and asphalt, from a distance it
looked like "woods overhanging mountains." Mighty engines raised water
from the Euphrates to care for the gardens. Attached to the hanging gardens was a magnificent palace of unequaled size and splendor. The outer
wall of this palace was no less than six miles in circumference. All its
gates were of brass. The interior decorations were beautiful, and included
a multitude of wonderful statues both of human beings and animals. For
eating and drinking there were numerous beautiful vessels of gold and
silver, and indeed every article for luxurious living which the known world
could supply. If Nebuchadnezzar was condemned by God for proudly
boasting of such an achievement surely this should be a warning to the
rest of mortals that the greatest things they can accomplish in a worldly
way are but paltry and transitory and afford little reason for pride. See
also Charles F. Pfeiffer (ed.), *The Biblical World*, pp. 124-32.

institutions in those days. The insane were allowed to wander as they wished without harm or hindrance, it being felt that they had been touched by the gods. For seven dreary years Nebuchadnezzar lived like an animal.

Finally, after many days Nebuchadnezzar with some faint glimmer of rationality left to him, although speechless, silently acknowledged the sovereignty of God by lifting up his eyes to heaven. The chastisement ended, the king's mind was restored. His first act was to praise God—to acknowledge His greatness and his own insignificance. Not only did God restore to him his reason, but the honor and glory of his kingdom as well. This time Nebuchadnezzar did not forget the lesson taught him. His last words appear to be those of a truly converted man.

5

BELSHAZZAR AND THE HANDWRITING ON THE WALL

(5:1-31)

THIS CHAPTER at one time furnished Bible critics with what they felt was a sure proof of the inaccuracy of Daniel. Berosus and Abydenus (heathen historians of Babylon) record the fact that Nabonidus was the last king of Babylon and that he had an honorable place assigned him after his surrender to the Persians.[1] Daniel, on the contrary, speaks of Belshazzar as the last king, and states that he met his death in the overthrow of Babylon. Archaeology has since proved both the heathen historians and the Bible to be accurate. Assyrian inscriptions found in 1854 by J. E. Taylor, British consul at Basra, reveal that Belshazzar was the son of Nabonidus, and that he reigned as joint king with his father.[2] This explains his offer (5:7 ff.) to make the one reading the inscription *"third* ruler in the kingdom." There were already two rulers—Belshazzar and his father.

[1]C. F. Keil, *Biblical Commentary on the Book of Daniel*, p. 164.
[2]G. Frederick Owen, *Archaeology and the Bible*, p. 141.

Why then is Nebuchadnezzar spoken of in this chapter as the "father" of Belshazzar? In the same sense that David is called "father" of Jesus in Luke 1:32—the meaning being simply that of an ancestor. It is thought that Belshazzar's mother, Nitocris, was the daughter of Nebuchadnezzar. "Belshazzar was a grandson of Nebuchadnezzar, and therefore called him his father 'in harmony with Semitic usage.' "[3]

Secular history states that the events of this chapter took place on one of the great festival days of the Babylonians,[4] so at first glance it does not seem strange that "Belshazzar made a great feast." But history also shows that for some three months Cyrus the Persian had been besieging the city of Babylon. So with this powerful army without his gates it seems that Belshazzar should have been fasting rather than feasting. His confidence however was in the mighty walls surrounding the city. According to Herodotus these walls were no less than 87 feet thick and 350 feet high. In addition there were 250 watchtowers which extended another 100 feet into the air.[5] Belshazzar felt sure that Babylon could never be captured. This chapter provides still another illustration of how quickly the security of the wicked can vanish.

At first the king drank with a thousand of his nobles. Later his wives and concubines joined the party. For an added thrill, Belshazzar ordered that the sacred vessels, carried from the temple in Jerusalem by Nebuchadnezzar years before, be brought forth. There was no question of necessity (as when David and his men ate the showbread

[3]Owen, p. 142. See also Merrill F. Unger, *Unger's Bible Dictionary*, p. 133.
[4]Herodotus, *Persian Wars*, I. 191.
[5]*Ibid.*, 178-79.

in the tabernacle—Mark 2:25-26). There was not even any special pleasure to be found in drinking from these vessels, because wine tastes no better in one goblet than another. The audacious act can only be considered as one of pure defiance of Jehovah, the God of Israel, since these vessels had been consecrated to His service.

To make the deed even more blasphemous, while they drank from these sacred utensils, they praised their own idol gods, perhaps with song or the offering of sacrifice. Jehovah God did not let such a challenge go unanswered.

THE HANDWRITING ON THE WALL (5:5-9)

God immediately spoke in judgment on this impious act —"in the same hour." This time His method was not a dream nor a miraculous deliverance as to Nebuchadnezzar, but in a very simple and quiet but effective way. Suddenly a hand appeared and began to write on the wall near the light. Such walls were usually filled with boasting inscriptions concerning the supposed prowess of the king. How fitting that in such a place should be recorded the doom of this wicked, God-hating rebel!

It must indeed have been shocking to see a hand, with no body attached, writing. In an instant the king was sobered. The hand was that of God—the same that wrote the two tables of the law for His people. Still why was the king so exceedingly fearful? Since he did not understand the writing, why did he not imagine that it contained something good about him? The answer is that his guilty conscience accused him at once. His "countenance" (Hebrew *ziv*, brightness) was changed from a look of gaiety to one of dreadful fear. One moment the life of the party, the next a stricken man. Thus quickly do God's judgments some-

times fall on the wicked. When He chooses God can bring
low the proudest sinner in a moment. So terrified was
Belshazzar that "the joints of his loin were loosed" ("the
vertebrae of his back") .[6] His knees smote together.

The king called for all his wise men but none could read
or interpret the mysterious handwriting. Apparently the
thought here expressed is that none could "read under-
standingly," for the words themselves were common ones.
Probably all the nobles could decipher them, but none
could understand the significance of these four simple
words.

DANIEL BROUGHT BEFORE THE KING (5:10-16)

Just at this time, the queen appeared on the scene, sug-
gesting Daniel as interpreter. This lady was evidently not
one of Belshazzar's wives, since these were already present.
From the respect with which he treated her, it seems a
reasonable conjecture that she was his mother, the daughter
of Nebuchadnezzar. The terms in which she described
Daniel were reminiscent of those used by Nebuchadnezzar
before his humbling (4:8-9). Daniel appears to have
dropped into obscurity after the latter's death. It is not
difficult to understand his aversion to holding any close
contact with such a man as Belshazzar. This illustrates the
sad fact that the ablest men are sometimes little recognized
while those far inferior hold high office.

However the king, who had formerly thought so little
of one who had been Nebuchadnezzar's chief minister, now
desperately turned to the noble old man of God. Hurriedly
explaining the situation to Daniel, he offered him a princely
reward if he could interpret the writing.

[6]Jamieson, Fausset and Brown, *Commentary*, IV, 408.

DANIEL'S INTERPRETATION (5:17-29)

Daniel's attitude toward Belshazzar, a man of the vilest character, was quite different from his affectionate interest in Nebuchadnezzar. He spurned the offer of this pusillanimous upstart. Little did Belshazzar then realize how worthless his fine proffer would soon be! Though rejecting the reward, Daniel nevertheless agreed to read the writing. Before doing so, however, he reminded the king of the experience of Nebuchadnezzar when God humbled him (chap. 4). Then he made a terrible indictment of Belshazzar. Three charges were laid against this wicked monarch:

1. His sin was not one of ignorance. He knew all the facts concerning Nebuchadnezzar's case, but failed to heed the object lesson, and did not humble his own proud heart. When God gives men light, He expects them to follow that illumination. Jesus Christ pronounced awful judgment on cities of His own day that refused to heed His mighty works, saying that it would be worse for them than for Sodom (Matt. 11:20-24). It was not that their moral depravity was worse than that of Sodom, but that with far more light they still remained unrepentant.. If Belshazzar was held accountable for the comparatively small amount of light given him, then what about people today, who not only have the complete Word of God, but also live in the glow of almost two thousand years of gospel preaching?

2. Beyond this, Belshazzar had impudently and impiously turned against almighty God and had gone out of his way to defy Him. Though God had so graciously given him all things—not alone his kingdom, but even his breath, his very life itself—yet he did not glorify God. Why are human beings granted an existence on this earth? "Man's chief

end is to glorify God, and to enjoy Him forever," truly speaks the *Westminster Shorter Catechism*. Belshazzar failed in that which was the chief end of man. Reader, what about you?

3. Belshazzar had worshiped idols and had praised them. While gross idol worship is in many countries today no longer a temptation, it is possible to make idols of other things than images of wood and stone. The first epistle of the Apostle John warns believers: "Little children, keep yourselves from idols" (5:21). Anything which is given the place in the heart that God alone should have—first place— becomes an idol. For such sins, God's judgment fell on Belshazzar.

The mysterious message itself consisted of four words, three different, one repeated: *Mene, mene, tekel, upharsin.* The words meant "numbered, numbered, weighed, divisions."[7] The perplexing question was: How should these words be understood? After the condemnation of Belshazzar, Daniel gave the interpretation. *Mene* (numbered) meant: "God hath numbered thy kingdom, and finished it." God had determined just how far to let the king proceed in his evil way, and that limit had now been reached. *Tekel* (weighed) signified: "Thou art weighed in the balances and found wanting." The picture is of balance scales. On one side was the man Belshazzar should have been in view of the blessings and privileges God had given him. On the other side was the man he actually proved to be—far, far too light! Belshazzar had great privileges, but had not fulfilled the corresponding responsibilities. *Peres* (the singular form of the plural *upharsin,* divisions)[8] meant: "Thy kingdom is divided and given to the Medes and Persians."

[7]Clarence Larkin, *The Book of Daniel,* p. 89.
[8]Jamieson, Fausset and Brown, IV, 410.

It might be thought that such an interpretation would have infuriated Belshazzar, but not so. Evidently he was too deeply convicted as to the justice of this divine sentence. The promised reward was given Daniel, but it was of small value. The gifts of a condemned king are worth little. Before the night had ended, his reign and power, his very life itself, had come to a final conclusion. Men today should reflect that the rewards of a condemned world are likewise of small worth. Yet many think nothing of eternal things, but instead burn out their lives attempting to obtain the fleeting popularity of this present world. "Love not the world, neither the things that are in the world. If any man love the world, the love of the Father is not in him. For all that is in the world, the lust of the flesh, and the lust of the eyes, and the pride of life, is not of the Father, but is of the world. And the world passeth away, and the lust thereof: but he that doeth the will of God abideth for ever" (I John 2:15-17).

THE AFTERMATH (5:30-31)

Early in the evening the handwriting on the wall appeared; just before morning light, the seemingly impregnable city fell. While the drunken Babylonians were carousing, Cyrus effected a plan relating to the Euphrates River which flowed under the mighty wall and through the city of Babylon. The river was temporarily diverted from its old course to a new channel. Then the army, guided by two deserters, marched into the city by the almost dry riverbed under the wall, threw open the gates, and suddenly captured Babylon.[9] That night Belshazzar was slain, and the divine prophecy quickly fulfilled.

[9]Herodotus, I. 191.

Darius the Mede (mentioned in 5:31) was apparently Gobryas, commanding general of Cyrus, appointed by him to be the governor of Babylon. He chose to take the title of Darius.[10] This name was evidently used on different occasions for various kings, just as Pharaoh had been used in Egypt and Caesar was later to be used in Rome.[11]

---

[10]Such an identification has been made by various commentators throughout the years, but all the evidence has been ably collected in John C. Whitcomb, *Darius the Mede.*

[11]The exact meaning of the name Darius is not known, but Gleason Archer states that it means "possibly . . . 'the royal one' " (*A Survey of Old Testament Introduction*, p. 373).

6

DANIEL IN THE LIONS' DEN

(6:1-28)

DANIEL'S POSITION UNDER DARIUS (6:1-3)

IN THE OPENING CHAPTER of the book, Daniel first appeared as a young boy. In this closing chapter of the historical section, Daniel is observed as an old man. Yet from first to last he is seen as the same faithful, courageous servant of God. Babylon fell about 538 B.C. Therefore when the events related in chapter 5 took place, Daniel must have been around eighty years of age. The present chapter records experiences which were his very shortly after the downfall of Babylon.

Darius now possessed a new realm to govern, so to better accomplish this task he divided the kingdom into one hundred twenty provinces, over each of which he set a prince, or *satrap*.[1] These one hundred twenty satraps were subordinate to three presidents[2] under the direct control of the king himself. The responsibility of the presidents was to oversee the affairs of the whole realm so that the interests

[1]"The governor of the greater provinces amongst the ancient Persians" (Gesenius, *Hebrew and Chaldee Lexicon*, p. 34).
[2]"A royal minister of the Persians" (Gesenius, p. 595).

73

of the king would not be damaged. Surprisingly enough, the first of these presidents chosen by Darius was none other than Daniel the prophet. Scripture does not say how he came into such favor with the new king. Probably Darius, knowing of the miraculous handwriting Daniel had interpreted, had first interviewed him through curiosity. Highly impressed with his sagacity and sterling character, he had immediately appointed Daniel to a position of great trust. This king certainly possessed at least one valuable trait—he knew a good man when he saw one! This is more than can be said for some modern rulers. Daniel certainly must have been vigorous in both body and mind to be able to handle such heavy responsibility at his advanced age.

Daniel's work obviously was very satisfactory to the king; Darius preferred him above all the other officials. Arrangements were made to place in his hand all the affairs of the kingdom. The reason for this is explained in the words "because an excellent spirit was in him." The working of the Holy Spirit of God in Daniel's life was manifest to all.

DANIEL'S ENEMIES AND THEIR PLOT
AGAINST HIM (6:4-9)

But there was one "fly in the ointment" to spoil this pleasant picture. The other presidents and princes hated Daniel. The cause for this hatred certainly could not have been any unjust or unfair treatment received by them, but purely their jealousy. They hated him because he was both great and good. When they learned of the king's plan to make Daniel supreme over all his affairs, they decided that the time had come to strike. First they sought painstakingly to find something wrong in Daniel's management of the king's business. If the slightest slip had been discovered,

these unscrupulous men would undoubtedly have so mag-
nified it as to make a mountain out of a molehill. But
nothing could be found "forasmuch as he was faithful."
Coming from one's enemies this is a tremendous testimony.
Daniel was an honest, faithful man, so there was no danger
of their finding any wrongdoing on his part. But beyond
this "neither was there any error or fault found in him."
He was not only faithful but also careful. He did not consider that honesty of heart would excuse him for careless,
shoddy work. An old writer said: "If a Christian man is a
shoeblack, he ought to be the best shoeblack in the parish."[3]
The world judges Christians not by their faith, which only
God can see, but by their conduct (James 2:18). How
many today could stand such a scrutiny as Daniel received
on this occasion?

Daniel's enemies were finally forced to the conclusion
that they would never be able to scrape up any charge
against him unless it would be something in connection
with his religion. They well knew he would obey the law
of his God regardless of anything else, so they decided the
only way to trap him would be to convict him of breaking
some law of the land which was contrary to the law of God.

In order to ruin Daniel, these evil men determined to
promulgate a new law—one designed not to be kept but to
be broken. Such a law is bound to be a poor one. To this
end they assembled together ("assembled hastily and tu-
multuously") before the king.[4] By the very suddenness of
their approach they took the king off guard so that without
thinking the matter through, he signed their law. How

[3]Quoted in Alexander Maclaren, *Expositions of Holy Scripture*, VI,
72.
[4]Jamieson, Fausset and Brown, *Commentary*, IV, 482.

many men have rushed into rash, foolish acts which they later bitterly regretted!

No doubt the conspirators represented to Darius that such a step was necessary to test the loyalty of newly acquired lands. Their opening statement was a lie: "All the presidents . . . have consulted together." Daniel, the chief president, was not present and certainly had not approved the proposal. The law was such as to appeal to the king's vanity and thus obtain his signature. People would have to make their requests to him, emphasizing his power and bringing him popularity as a public benefactor. And once the decree was signed it became an established law of the Medes and Persians which, unlike those of the Babylonians, could not be broken even by the king himself. How foolish to think that fallible legislators can make infallible laws. All men are human and therefore subject to error. So it is true of individuals, as well as of nations, that the one who never changes is guilty of either foolishness or pride. This law, sad to say, was only one of many that have since been passed in various lands, not for the good of the realm, but solely for the purpose of persecution. In a somewhat similar situation, the Apostle Peter's voice rang out with the words "We ought to obey God rather than men" (Acts 5:29). The person who refuses to obey an unrighteous law "and unresistingly accepts the appointed penalty . . . is not properly regarded as a lawbreaker."[5] In a modern application, beyond the matter of unrighteous laws, Christians should be willing to go against the customs of the day, no matter how widespread, if such are contradictory to the commands of Christ. Such matters truly test the faith of professed believers.

[5]Maclaren, p. 74.

DANIEL'S "OBEDIENT DISOBEDIENCE"[6] (6:10-15)

Only after the decree was signed did Daniel learn of the iniquitous law. There were several alternatives he could have taken. He could of course have discontinued all his prayers for thirty days. He could have hidden while praying. He could have made a bold public show. He did none of these. He simply followed his usual custom of praying three times daily with his face toward the holy city (in accordance with the words of Solomon, as found in I Kings 8:29 ff.). He did not especially open the windows ("his windows being open") in order to make a spectacle of what he was doing. That would have seemed vain bravado. He did not close them to hide his actions. That would have smacked of cowardice. Incidentally, if Daniel, busy as he was at the head of a great empire with its many affairs, could find time to pray three times a day, have God's children now any real cause to claim that they are too busy to pray?

Once again Daniel's evil enemies assembled, this time to spy on him. As soon as they observed him praying, they rushed to the king to make their accusation. First reminding the king of the law previously signed, they then informed him of one who had broken it—"that Daniel." Those two simple words revealed their bitter antagonism.

At last the foolish king saw through the plot. He was "sore displeased." With Daniel? No, with himself. He realized how vain and weak he had been to sign such a decree. In this evil world with its many temptations, to be weak is often the same as to be wicked, so far as result is concerned.

Daniel needed no advocate to argue his cause. The king

[6]*Ibid.,* p. 73.

himself became his lawyer, and for the balance of the day
sought some loophole whereby he could circumvent the
execrable law. It is clear that he already had a deep affec-
tion for Daniel, as he "set his heart on Daniel to deliver
him," and to this end "he laboured till the going down of
the sun." All was to no avail—the law had to be enforced.

DANIEL'S PUNISHMENT AND HIS DELIVERANCE
(6:16-24)

Finally the king acknowledged failure and gave the order
that Daniel should be cast into the lions' den. He admitted
that the sole reason for Daniel's punishment was that the
latter "continually" served his God, and with hopeful words
(which he found hardly convincing himself) he sought to
encourage the prophet. After Daniel was cast in, the mouth
of the den was covered with a stone, and the seals of the
king and his lords were placed upon it. Who rested better
that night? The king in his palace, or the prophet in the
den? It is far better to suffer injustice than to do injustice.
Very early, after a sleepless night, Darius hastened to seek
Daniel at the den.

The king had previously expressed faith that Daniel's
God would deliver him, but his belief was mingled with
doubt. Now he hoped for the best but evidently feared the
worst. Apparently it was dark in the den, and the king
could not at first tell whether Daniel was alive or dead.
When he cried "with a lamentable voice," however, Daniel
immediately answered, using the customary form of salu-
tation to the monarch. Then continuing, Daniel gave the
story of his deliverance. God had sent an angel to seal the
mouths of the lions. This miraculous aid was granted because of his innocency before God. He did not claim sinless

perfection, but he did insist that he was innocent of any real wrongdoing, and had done no actual harm to the king, even though he had disobeyed the unfair decree.

The king gladly received Daniel from the den. The real reason behind his supernatural deliverance is explained in verse 23: "No manner of hurt was found upon him, because he believed in his God." The writer of Hebrews evidently referred to this incident when he stated that "through faith [some] . . . stopped the mouths of lions" (Heb. 11:33).

Darius did one thing more. After Daniel was free, he proceeded to punish the wicked men who had plotted against the righteous prophet. According to Persian custom, they with their families were punished. (It should be noted that the punishment of the families of criminals was expressly forbidden by the Mosaic law; cf. Deut. 24:16; II Kings 14:6.) To these men it had not been enough to ruin Daniel—they had determined to take his very life. The final result was that Daniel escaped and they themselves suffered the terrible doom they had so cruelly planned for him. The evidence is conclusive that it was not because of lack of hunger the beasts did not consume Daniel. They tore these villains to shreds even before their bodies came to rest on the floor of the den.

DARIUS' PROCLAMATION (6:25-28)

A vastly superior decree was then issued by the king. It is indeed stronger than that of Nebuchadnezzar, recorded in 3:29. Nebuchadnezzar only commanded that men should not say anything against the true God—a negative edict. Darius commanded them to tremble and fear before God—a positive decree. It is to be hoped that both Darius and

Nebuchadnezzar really learned their lessons and were truly converted.

The closing picture of Daniel's life is to be found in verse 28. He prospered. The one who trusts God will always prosper, spiritually if not materially (Ps. 1:3). Though quite old at the time of the lions' den incident, the prophet had still further years of usefulness—on into the full reign of King Cyrus. The last prophecy of his book was recorded in the third year of Cyrus (10:1).

In the persecution of faithful Daniel, some have seen a foreshadowing of the persecution and deliverance of the faithful Israelites of the "last days," who will likewise refuse to bow down and worship the "beast-king" of that period.[7] Chapter 11 contains direct prophecy concerning this.

[7]A. C. Gaebelein, *The Prophet Daniel*, p. 68.

PART TWO

PROPHETICAL SECTION

(7:1—12:13)

7

THE VISION OF THE FOUR BEASTS AND THE LITTLE HORN

(7:1-28)

DANIEL'S VISION (7:1-14)

THIS VISION WAS GRANTED Daniel during "the first year of Belshazzar king of Babylon," so chronologically this chapter comes before chapters 5 and 6. Instead of interpreting the dream of another, as he had done previously, Daniel was now given one of his own. There is little room for imagination, so far as the meaning of the dream is concerned, for it was immediately interpreted for the prophet. Generally speaking, it covered the same ground as Nebuchadnezzar's vision of chapter 2, but with certain significant differences and additions.

The symbolism used was decidedly different. Nebuchadnezzar, the *natural* man (I Cor. 2:14), saw the four great world kingdoms represented in their external *political* aspect as a splendid and majestic image of a colossal man. Daniel, the *spiritual* man (I Cor. 2:15), saw these same four kingdoms as four dreadful, ravenous beasts, speaking of the *moral* aspect of these world empires. Nebuchadnezzar saw Christ as a stone, at first small, then growing exceedingly large. Daniel saw Him in a direct way as the glorified Son of Man coming to set up His everlasting kingdom on the earth. Daniel saw a representation of the Antichrist—the evil king of the last days—a detail not shown to Nebuchadnezzar at all.

After the vision had been given Daniel he was constrained to "tell the sum," to give a summary, for the benefit of his people and also for the Babylonians, since the text continues in the Aramaic language through this chapter. He also "wrote the dream," so that the record of it might be preserved for future generations.

His night vision opened with a view of the "great sea," the term then used for what we call the Mediterranean Sea (Num. 34:6-7; Joshua 15:47). Upon the sea the "four winds of heaven" were striving. Then in succession four ferocious beasts arose from the sea. Each of the four vast empires represented by these beasts eventually bordered on the Mediterranean Sea, Rome finally controlling its entire coast. Thus it is quite fitting to picture these four kingdoms as arising from this sea. Beyond this, the sea in biblical symbolism represents "peoples, and multitudes, and nations, and tongues" (Rev. 17:15; see also Luke 21:25; Isa. 57:20). "The great sea, agitated by tempests, is a fitting emblem of the perpetual turmoil, restlessness, and commotions out of which have emerged the four great world empires."[1] The four winds of heaven speak of the unseen but active agency of God, as He works behind the scenes in the affairs of our world. Wind is sometimes used in the Bible to symbolize the Holy Spirit (e.g., John 3:8). As a matter

[1]Jamieson, Fausset and Brown, *Commentary*, IV, 424.

of fact in both the Hebrew and Greek languages the same
word means "breath," "wind" and "spirit."[2]

The four beasts are said in verse 17 to be "four kings."
Later however, in verse 23, the fourth beast is identified as
the "fourth kingdom." Evidently each refers to an empire,
and at the same time to one outstanding king in that empire. In chapter 2 Nebuchadnezzar himself was said to be
the "head of gold" (2:38). Cyrus and Alexander far overshadowed other kings of the Persian and Greek empires.
The most notable king of the fourth empire is yet to come—
the beast-king of Revelation 13.

Daniel's vision clearly centers around these four beasts.
The first was like a lion, except that it also had eagle's
wings. This beast represents Babylon.[3] The lion speaks of
its strength, courage and ferocity.[4] The wings symbolize
the swiftness of its movements during its conquests. (In
Ezek. 17 the eagle itself is used to represent Babylon.) As
Daniel watched, the wings were plucked from this lion, and
it was made to stand on its hind legs only. Its heart was
changed to that of a man. One noted English king, famed
for his bravery, was called "the lion-hearted." Here instead
of a man with a lion's heart there is a lion with a man's
heart. All of this clearly tells of the once strong and swift
lion becoming clumsy and cowardly. This happened to
Babylon in the days of Belshazzar.

[2]The Hebrew word *ruach* is translated in the AV as breath 28 times,
wind 90 times, and Spirit 232 times (see Robert Young, *Analytical Concordance to the Bible*). The Greek word *pneuma* has the same range of
meaning (see W. E. Vine, *Expository Dictionary of New Testament
Words*, IV, 62).

[3]"Elsewhere Nebuchadnezzar is likened to a lion in strength (Jer. 4:7;
5:6; 49:19; 50:17) and to an eagle for swiftness (Jer. 48:40; 49:22; Lam.
4:19; Hab. 1:8; Ezek. 17:3, 12; 27:2)" (William Edward Biederwolf,
The Millennium Bible, p. 206).

[4]Merrill F. Unger, *Unger's Bible Dictionary*, p. 662.

The second beast was like a bear. The bear's predominant qualities are thought to be strength, austerity and cruelty.[5] This fitly symbolizes the Medo-Persian Empire. This bear "raised up itself on one side," or "raised up one dominion" (ASV, margin). The Medo-Persian Empire was formed through a combination of two nations—Media, the older, and Persia, the more modern. Very soon Persia gained the ascendancy over Media. That the bear had ravaged the lion was evident for "it had three ribs in the mouth of it between the teeth of it." These very likely were the three chief cities of Babylon—Ecbatana, Borsippa and Babylon itself. All of these were captured by the armies of Cyrus.[6] These ribs then urged the bear to extend its dominion yet farther: "Arise, devour much flesh."

Next appeared an animal like a leopard, but possessing in addition four wings and four heads.[7] This leopard symbolizes the Grecian Empire. Though smaller than the lion, the leopard is very swift and cruel, jumping from a hiding place on its victim.[8] Four wings indicate great rapidity of conquest, which was fulfilled under the leadership of Alexander the Great. His army was noted for its extreme mobility. The four heads obviously refer to the four sections into which Alexander's empire was divided after his early death. The four sections came under the control of his four leading generals. The Bible says of this empire that "dominion was given to it." Alexander was a military genius, and doubtless felt that his victories came entirely by his own power and ability. But had not God given the victory to him, he could have accomplished nothing.

[5]Jamieson, Fausset and Brown, IV, 418.
[6]H. A. Ironside, *Lectures on Daniel the Prophet*, p. 126.
[7]So taken "by common consent" (Biederwolf, p. 207).
[8]Jamieson, Fausset and Brown, *ibid.*

The greater part of the chapter is occupied with the fourth beast, which represented the Roman Empire.[9] An exact description is not given of this creature other than that it was "diverse from all the others." The Apostle John (Rev. 13:1) apparently saw this same beast, and he described it as being like a leopard, with bear's feet and a lion's mouth. It was therefore a composite of the other three. Rome always claimed that it did not destroy the cultures it conquered but incorporated them into its own.[10] This animal was also much greater in power than the others had been. It was "dreadful, and terrible, and strong exceedingly." The full, divine explanation of these features is to be found in verse 23.

Daniel witnessed a strange and weird sight in connection with this fourth beast. On its head were ten horns. Suddenly another "little horn" began to grow up among the original ones. It should be carefully observed that this event abruptly advanced the prophetic picture from the opening stage of the Roman Empire to the very closing scene of the world drama, the same time period represented in Nebuchadnezzar's dream by the feet and ten toes of the great image. So between verses 7 and 8 is to be found again the "great parenthesis" noted in chapter 2. What was to transpire during this interim? The answer is to be found in Ephesians 3:3-6.

While Daniel watched, the "little horn" (the horn symbolizes power and authority in Bible usage)[11] overcame three of the other horns, so that they were "plucked up by

[9]"This beast is acknowledged by all to refer to the same kingdom as that represented by the 'legs of iron' in the vision of 2:40" (Biederwolf, p. 207).
[10]Ironside, pp. 128-29.
[11]See Deut. 33:17; I Sam. 2:1; Ps. 75:5, 10; Jer. 48:25.

the roots." The little horn itself is described as having "eyes like the eyes of a man, and a mouth speaking great things." Eyes speak of intelligence.[12] The mouth was speaking great blasphemies against God (v. 25).

As Daniel further observed, he saw thrones "cast down." This expression refers to the Oriental custom of preparing a throne by "casting down" pillows and cushions. The picture, therefore, is of thrones being placed (ASV), rather than torn down as it might at first seem. The Ancient of Days was seated. The eternal God prepared for judgment on Gentile world dominion. The way in which He is described is quite reminiscent of the picture of Christ in Revelation 1. The hair like "snow" and "wool" probably refers not to white hair, such as an old man might possess, as that is the result of decay, but rather to the radiance that streamed from Him, as in the transfiguration scene (Matt. 17:2). Of the Messiah it is said: "Thou hast the dew of thy youth" (Ps. 110:3). He is not One who is eternally old but eternally young! The "fiery flame," the "burning fire" and the "fiery stream" which Daniel saw, symbolize both purity and judgment.[13] This tremendous scene is parallel to Christ's picture of the "judgment of the nations" in the Olivet discourse (Matt. 25:31-46).

Finally Daniel saw the "little horn" come to his doom, and the beast itself (the Roman Empire) was destroyed. The other beasts, when overcome, had their dominion taken from them but "their lives were prolonged." In other words, each of them was absorbed into the new empire which followed. The last beast, however, met a different fate. When his doom came there was final destruction.

[12]See Ezek. 1:18; Zech. 3:9; Rev. 4:6, 8; 5:6.
[13]Unger, p. 365.

As the vision came to an end, Daniel was given a close-up of the second advent of the incarnate Christ returning to the earth to rule and to reign (cf. Matt. 26:64). Unlike the former kingdoms, which passed away, the promise is made that His kingdom shall stand forever.

THE INTERPRETATION (7:15-28)

Daniel was at first deeply troubled about this vision, part of which, at least, he understood very little. He turned and spoke to one standing by, probably an angel, asking for an interpretation. It is of interest to note that the prophet speaks of "my spirit in the midst [sheath] of my body." As a scabbard sheathes the sword, so the body sheathes the soul, or spirit. In response to Daniel's request the interpretation was made known, and assurance was given him that although these godless empires must run their course, eventually "the saints shall possess the kingdom." While the specific reference is doubtless to the saints among Daniel's people who will pass triumphantly through the great tribulation, it is likewise true that all of Christ's own will reign with Him (II Tim. 2:12).

The brief explanation of verses 17-18 evidently did not fully satisfy Daniel. He still wanted to know more about the awe-inspiring fourth beast and the mysterious "little horn." Students of prophecy today can well be thankful for Daniel's persistent curiosity. Verses 21-22 add further information as to what Daniel had previously seen regarding this "little horn" and his evildoing. He not only conquered other horns, but also made war with God's saints and overcame them until the time of his downfall.

Between verses 23 and 24 the "great parenthesis" is again to be found. Verse 23 tells of the rise of the fourth kingdom, the Roman Empire. Verse 24 speaks of a time when ten kings (represented by the ten horns) will arise out of the territory once controlled by Rome. The "little horn" is a ruler who will be different from the other kings and will subdue three of them. Undoubtedly he is the "beast-king" of Revelation 13 and 17—popularly called the Antichrist.[14]

Verse 25 reveals some of the things this evil man will do during the yet future great tribulation: blaspheme God, try to change God's appointed seasons and laws, hold sway over the tribulation saints for a definite period. This is stated to be "a time and times and the dividing of time," in other words, three and a half years (cf. 4:16, 23). These three and a half years represent the truly intensive portion of the tribulation period—the last half of the seventieth "week" of Daniel 9. At the beginning of this "week" of years Antichrist will make a treaty with the Jews, but in the middle of the period will break the treaty and demand worship for himself. When the Jews refuse to perform such worship, the great tribulation will begin.

In spite of this "little horn's" fierceness, however, God's judgment upon him is settled. Eventually he will be destroyed, and the saints whom he persecuted will inherit the kingdom. The closing words of the angel-interpreter were: "Hitherto is the end of the matter." Daniel still did not fully understand the meaning of the vision, but he "kept

[14]Some expositors feel that the second beast of Revelation 13—"the beast . . . out of the earth" (v. 11)—should be called the Antichrist (see the Scofield Reference Bible, pp. 1342-43, n). While he is *an* antichrist without doubt, he seems to be a lesser figure, sort of a religious assistant to the political ruler. He is called elsewhere in Revelation "the false prophet." He is mentioned only in the book of Revelation whereas the political ruler is mentioned in many books of both Old and New Testaments. It seems to me he is *the* Antichrist (I John 2:18) and I will thus denominate him in the rest of this volume.

the matter in his heart." It is well for us to do likewise. "The Holy Spirit intended much more to be understood by Daniel's words than Daniel himself understood. We are not to limit the significance of prophecies to what the prophets themselves understood (I Peter 1:11-12)."[15]

[15]Jamieson, Fausset and Brown, IV, 424.

8

THE VISION OF THE RAM AND THE ROUGH GOAT

(8:1-27)

DANIEL'S VISION (8:1-14)

THIS VISION WAS GRANTED to Daniel during the third year of the reign of King Belshazzar, some two years after that of chapter 7. Evidently the time was shortly before the fall of Babylon, described in chapter 5. Daniel was in Shushan, the capital of the province of Elam. (Elam was west of Persia proper, east of Babylon, and south of Media.) At the time of Daniel's visitation, the city was overshadowed by Babylon, but later it was to become the capital city of Cyrus. Daniel was in the palace, but in the vision itself he was transported to the banks of the river Ulai, a stream flowing near the city.

Whereas in his earlier vision Daniel had observed four beasts, he now saw but two. The first of these was a ram with two horns, one of which was much longer than the other. This ram pushed in all directions and no power was able to stop him. Verse 20 leaves no doubt as to what this ram symbolized: "The ram which thou sawest having two horns are the kings of Media and Persia."

Just as the ram seemed to be absolutely supreme, a formidable enemy appeared to challenge him. This enemy was a rough he-goat, equipped with one very large horn which grew between his eyes. He was so swift that his feet "touched not the ground." Attacking the hitherto victorious ram, he completely conquered him.

After this the goat became exceedingly great, but at the moment of his greatest strength, a surprising change took place. The large horn was broken, and four "notable" horns came up in its place, extending "toward the four winds of heaven."

Again there is an inspired interpretation. According to verses 21-22, the goat represented Greece. The original great horn was the "first king," Alexander the Great. At his downfall his empire, it was prophesied, would be divided into four parts, none of which would be powerful as the original kingdom. This was strikingly fulfilled, even though the prophecy was written before the actual fall of Babylon. At Alexander's untimely death, after a brief period of bickering, his empire was divided into four sections, each going to one of his leading generals. This division was made more than two hundred years subsequent to Daniel's prophecy. About 300 B.C. Greece went to Cassander; Asia Minor (including Syria) to Seleucus; Egypt to Ptolemy; and the eastern section of the empire to Lysimachus.

From one of these "horns," there arose a "little horn." Since it is clearly stated that the four symbolized kingdoms would originate from the division of Alexander's empire, this little horn must represent a ruler who would arise in one of those divisions. Bible students are greatly divided when it comes to identifying this little horn. Some consider it to be unquestionably identical with the little horn of chapter 7.[1] Others distinguish the two, holding that the reference in chapter 7 is to the Antichrist, while this chapter refers to another leading character of the last days—the "Assyrian" of Isaiah's prophecy.[2] Most often the little horn of chapter 8 has been identified with Antiochus Epiphanes, who reigned over the Syrian branch of the former Greek Empire about 175 B.C.[3] This personage is certainly pictured in a prophetic way in Daniel 11:21-35. He is there called "a vile person," and has well been termed the Antichrist of the Old Testament period. At first he sought by flatteries to gain the favor of the Jews, but when that failed, he turned to become the bitter persecutor of the Hebrews. During the course of his career he desecrated the temple at Jerusalem, erecting an idolatrous altar upon the altar of burnt offerings, and sacrificing a sow upon it. He sacked Jerusalem, slaying 80,000 people.[4] Just at the time things looked the blackest for God's ancient people, a heroic family, the Maccabees, appeared to lead the Jews against Antiochus. Under their leadership victory was finally attained, and the temple cleansed.

In attempting to arrive at a conclusion in this matter, certain factors seem to be clear: (1) The "little horn" of Daniel 8:9 *is* different from that of 7:8. The latter arose from the Roman Empire, and that in the "last days"; the former from a part of the Greek Empire shortly before the Roman conquest—"in the latter time of their kingdom"

[1]William L. Pettingill, *Simple Studies in Daniel,* p. 78.

[2]H. A. Ironside, *Lectures on Daniel the Prophet,* p. 150; A. C. Gaebelein, *The Prophet Daniel,* p. 108.

[3]Jamieson, Fausset and Brown, *Commentary,* IV, 426 ff. H. D. M. Spence and Joseph S. Exell (eds.), *Pulpit Commentary,* XIII, 241 ff.; C. F. Keil, *Biblical Commentary on the Book of Daniel,* p. 295.

[4]Josephus, *Antiquities of the Jews,* XII. 5; also II Maccabees 1; II Maccabees 5.

(v. 23). (2) Antiochus well fulfills the terms of the prophecy; however the language of the divine interpretation seems to go beyond anything that could be said of him. Evidently there is a double fulfillment, as in other prophetic Scriptures.[5] The direct reference is to Antiochus Epiphanes, but he foreshadows and is a type of the Antichrist of the last days, and the complete fulfillment will yet be seen in this latter personage.

Having settled this problem, the rest of the passage, though difficult, is not impossible to understand. The little horn soon "waxed exceeding great . . . toward the pleasant land"—a reference to Palestine, pleasant because it is the land of God's choosing. Verse 10 is called by Scofield "the most difficult [passage] in prophecy."[6] He suggests that it has been fulfilled in Antiochus, and will be fulfilled in the "beast-king" of the future in the "awful blasphemy" of their words and claims. The little horn magnifies himself "even to the prince of the host," or in other words against the Messiah. Literally, "the host was given up to him." This speaks of the power and success of both Antiochus and Antichrist. The 2,300 days of verse 14 are the time predicted for the period of Antiochus' desecrations—a bit more than six years. The cleansing was then accomplished by Judas Maccabeus. Speculating that each day represented a year (year-day theory), William Miller in the nineteenth century attempted to arrive at the date of the second advent of Christ.[7] Time proved his theory to be a mere figment of fancy. Actually this portion of the prophecy seems to have been completely fulfilled in the days of Antiochus

[5]Joseph Angus, *The Bible Handbook*, p. 237.
[6]C. I. Scofield, Scofield Reference Bible, p. 912, n.
[7]Ironside, p. 152.

and has no reference to the Messiah either direct or indirect.

THE INTERPRETATION (8:15-27)

When the vision had been concluded, Daniel earnestly sought for its meaning. We should do the same. There suddenly appeared before him One like a man. This "man" must surely have been the preincarnate Christ, for only He could command the mighty Gabriel, who was told to give Daniel the interpretation.

As the angel approached him, Daniel fell down in fear. He was told that the vision was to be for a future time— "the time of the end." This expression can be applied both to the time of Antiochus and to the last days before the Lord's return. Overcome by the splendor of the angelic minister, Daniel remained stunned on the earth, in a trancelike condition. Gabriel raised him up and strengthened him. He then gave the prophet an explanation of what he had seen, adding further information about the little horn. He was to be a man "of fierce countenance," and also would possess the ability to "understand dark sentences" or, better, "artifices." Along with his various crafty plans, this person, it was said, would possess mighty power, "but not by his own power." In the case of Antichrist, this will be fulfilled in the ten kings contributing their power to him. Until the time set for his judgment, he will prosper in his evil course. He will "destroy the mighty and the holy people"—a reference to the Jews. Not only by war, but also by peace does he destroy his enemies. By trickery and political maneuvering he gains more and more authority, finally standing up not merely against Israel but also against Israel's God and Messiah—the Prince of princes. In

the end he is "broken without hand." Antiochus Epiphanes, at the end of his life, was destroyed by a special
visitation from God. While advancing on the Maccabees,
he met a horrible death by worms and ulcers (quite similar
to the judgment of God on Herod Agrippa I, as described
in Acts 12).[8] The Antichrist will be smitten by Christ
Himself at His return (II Thess. 2:8).

As for the vision, Daniel was told to close it, since it was
"for many days." If we do not yet fully understand it, it
may perhaps be because the time for God's full opening of
the seal has not yet arrived.

The experience took its toll upon Daniel physically. As
he pondered on the terrible things to take place upon his
people, he was sick for "certain days." However as soon as
possible he arose, as he was engaged in some sort of business for the king. His final feeling about the matter was
one of astonishment and lack of understanding.

[8]II Maccabees 9.

9

DANIEL'S PRAYER AND THE VISION OF THE SEVENTY WEEKS
(9:1-27)

DANIEL'S PRAYER (9:1-19)

CHAPTER 9 TOOK PLACE after the fall of Babylon and in the first year of the reign of Darius—about the same time as chapter 6. This was 537 B.C., just sixty-nine years after Daniel had been carried captive to Babylon and one year before Cyrus permitted the Jews to return to Jerusalem.

The chapter opens with the interesting information that Daniel was not only a prophet in his own right but also a student of prophecy. He was studying the Word of God— "*the* books" (ASV). Chapter 6 reveals that even when exceedingly busy, Daniel found time to pray each day at morning, noon and night. This chapter shows that he also found time to study the Bible. How much more should modern believers do the same! He had only a portion of the Bible; we have the whole.

While reading in the book of Jeremiah, Daniel learned that seventy years were to be accomplished in the desolation of Jerusalem (see Jer. 25:9-11; 29:10). It is evident that he was studying prophecy not simply to satisfy his curiosity by learning something new and startling. His knowledge in the field had an immediate effect on his life. Realizing that he and his people were not in proper spiritual condition for the fulfillment of this prophecy, he began at once to intercede with God. His prayer is given at considerable length (vv. 3-19) and is deserving of careful attention.

First, there was confession of sin and acknowledgment of God's righteousness (vv. 3-14). Describing his experience Daniel wrote, I "made my confession." Though not personally guilty of the sin mentioned, nevertheless Daniel in confessing the sin of the nation made the confession his own. He felt that he, as a member of the nation, was in part responsible for its deeds.

Daniel began by vindicating God and admitting that Israel's condition was not at all the result of any failure on God's part to keep His promises. Two grievous sins had been committed by the nation. The people had disobeyed the law of God, even though it had been divinely revealed to them. Then they had refused to listen to the prophets sent by God to warn them. God had been perfectly righteous in His judgments on unheeding Israel. No excuse could be offered—Israel could only stand before God with "confusion of face," with guilt written all over their countenance. But though man may be faithless, God is always faithful. Daniel knew Him as a God of "mercies and forgiveness." Because all Israel had sinned, they were finally reaping the very curses God had recorded in the books of Moses. Saddest of all, even after terrible chastisement had come, the people had not truly turned back to God to seek His mercy.

After the confession, Daniel made his petition and request to God (vv. 15-19). He reminded the Lord of a previous occasion when He had given deliverance to Israel from their captivity and bondage in Egypt. Then he prayed that God would again turn in mercy instead of judgment to Jerusalem. This request was made for the Lord's sake—so that glory might redound to His name. Daniel reached the highest ground of all, asking for blessings not for his own sake, or even for Israel's sake, but for the Lord's sake—so that His name might be glorified, as the nations saw the great things He would do.

The prayer came to its end with a beautiful and fervent plea for God to work without delay—not because Daniel and his people in any sense deserved it, but because of God's grace.

The Vision of the Seventy Weeks (9:20-27)

While Daniel was still at prayer, the answer came. The angel Gabriel, who had previously appeared to Daniel at the river Ulai (8:16), was caused to fly swiftly to the prophet, touching him, while he was yet praying, to attract his attention. This same Gabriel, used then to predict the time of Messiah's coming, was later sent to announce His actual advent, as recorded in Luke 1. Daniel mentioned the time when the revelation was given to him—"about the time of the evening oblation"—about three P.M. It is beautiful to observe that although the evening oblation had not been offered for many years, due to the destruction of the temple at Jerusalem, Daniel still recalled the hour and offered prayers at that time.

Gabriel first explained to Daniel why he had come to visit him. Even as Daniel started to pray, God had sent the angel with the answer. Heaven is evidently not distant from earth for those who possess spiritual bodies. Daniel was said to be a man "greatly beloved" by God. The literal Hebrew is "man of desires." God desired him, delighted in him. The New Testament speaks of an apostle, who late in life was given a vision quite similar to Daniel's, as "the disciple whom Jesus loved." Though God's great love extends to all men, yet He loves in a special way those who walk in close fellowship with Him, and to such He delights to reveal His secrets.

Some confusion has resulted in the minds of Bible students because of the translation "weeks" in verse 24: "seventy weeks are determined." The word used in the original text of Scripture does not mean a week of days, but a group of seven of anything—a heptad.[1] (Our word *dozen* meaning twelve of anything is similar in nature.) Daniel was simply told that "seventy sevens are determined [cut out]." He had perhaps been thinking that in seventy years' time from the fall of Jerusalem, the wonderful Messianic kingdom was to be given to Israel. It appears that some of the Jews of that day had this idea. But God told him clearly that it would not take seventy years but seven times seventy to complete His wonderful work with Israel. The figure is perhaps that from the quarry of time God had, as it were, cut out 490 years for His further dealings with Israel. The fact that He calls Israel "thy people" is not an indication of His disowning them, but rather shows that Daniel in his intercession was recognized by God as the great advocate and representative for Israel.

The things which were to be accomplished in these 490

---

[1] The Hebrew word is *shabua.* Gesenius defines it as "a hebdomed, septenary number" (*Hebrew and Chaldee Lexicon,* p. 800).

years should be carefully observed. This period would be required (1) "to finish the transgression" or "restrain the transgression" (ASV, margin). The expression literally means "to shut up," signifying, in other words, to remove Israel's transgression from God's sight. (2) "To make an end of sins," or "to seal up sins" (ASV, margin), the completion of the course of sin. (3) "To make reconciliation for iniquity." The Old Testament word here used is the Hebrew *kaphar* often rendered "atonement" in the Authorized Version. Literally it means "to cover" sin. (4) "To bring in everlasting righteousness"—a real "enduring peace." (5) "To seal up the vision and prophecy [prophet, ASV, margin]," to bring to a conclusion by their fulfillment not only the various prophecies but the prophetic office itself. (6) "To anoint the most Holy [a most holy place, ASV, margin]." This is not a reference to Christ, as the Hebrew expression is always used of places not of persons.[2] The statement concerns the most holy place in the temple and its consecration again after its pollution by the beast-king in the last days. Once more, as when Solomon dedicated the temple of old, there will be an outpouring of the Shekinah glory of God (I Kings 8:10-11).

These six things have never yet been done, so obviously the time period of the seventy sevens has still not been completed. Before dealing with this problem it is best to study the divine elaboration as set forth in verses 25-26. Here the 490 years are divided into three sections: (1) "seven weeks"—49 years; (2) "threescore and two weeks" —434 years; (3) "one week"—7 years. Certain important things are prophesied as occurring during these three periods.

[2]Cf. its various uses as shown in Robert Young, *Analytical Concordance to the Bible*, p. 488.

The total length of time from the command to restore and rebuild Jerusalem down to Messiah the Prince is said to be 483 years (69 weeks of years). Sir Robert Anderson in his monumental work *The Coming Prince* has carefully worked out the chronology of this period. He begins by showing that only one decree was ever issued to rebuild Jerusalem—the one given Nehemiah by Artaxerxes (Neh. 2:1-8), the date of which was 445 B.C., on the first of Nisan, March 14. On the basis of a prophetic year of 360 days, the 69 weeks of years would equal 173,880 days. These would end on April 6, A.D. 32, the probable date of Christ's triumphal entry into Jerusalem.[3] Other scholars by a different computation figure the time as ending at the birth of Christ or at His baptism.[4] Be that as it may, the prophecy clearly predicted in an accurate and exact way the time of the first coming of Christ.

During the first period of 49 years, it is said that "the street shall be built again, and the wall, even in troublous times." The fulfillment of this prophecy is recorded by Nehemiah. After this there was to follow a second period of 434 years ("threescore and two weeks") about which there is no prediction, except that at the conclusion "Messiah shall be cut off, but not for himself." These years apparently concluded at the time of the triumphal entry into Jerusalem. It was then literally fulfilled that "after this" the Lord Jesus was "cut off, but not for himself." The literal translation of the latter expression is "shall have nothing" (ASV). He did indeed have nothing—"nothing, that is, which rightly was His."[5]

[3]Sir Robert Anderson, *The Coming Prince*, pp. 127-29.
[4]William Edward Biederwolf, *The Millennium Bible*, pp. 220-21.
[5]C. I. Scofield, The Scofield Reference Bible, p. 915.

Once again a great parenthesis[6] occurs between the fulfillment of verse 26 and that of verse 27. All that is said about the present lengthy dispensation in which we now live is to be found in the latter part of verse 26. At some time following the "cutting off" of Messiah—the crucifixion —"the people of the prince that shall come shall destroy the city and the sanctuary; and the end thereof shall be with a flood, and unto the end of the war desolations are determined." The fulfillment of this prophecy is easily found in history. In A.D. 70 the Roman legions, led by Titus, destroyed the city of Jerusalem and the temple. The flood possibly refers poetically to a "flood" of war (for similar uses of the term, see Isa. 8:7-8; 28:18; Ps. 90:5). It is of great significance to note that it is not said "the prince" shall destroy the city. The statement explicitly affirms that "the people of the prince that shall come shall destroy the city and the sanctuary." "The prince" here referred to is none other than the beast-king (or Antichrist) of the last days. He did not destroy Jerusalem in A.D. 70 as he was not then living on the earth. But his people—the Romans—did. The Antichrist will be the ruler of the reconstituted Roman Empire.

The last sentence in the verse describes the course of this age from A.D. 70 to its conclusion: "Unto the end wars and desolations are determined" (literal rendering).[7] Sad to say, wars and desolations are to be expected throughout this present dispensation until the "times of the Gentiles" are forever concluded.

With the rejection of the Messiah, God's "prophetic clock" stopped ticking for Israel, so to speak. Some day,

[6]See pp. 43, 87.
[7]Scofield, *ibid.*

however, it will commence again and the final week of years will then be fulfilled. When this will be is not revealed. It is simply said that "he [the future Roman prince] shall confirm the [a] covenant with many for one week." In other words, Antichrist will make a covenant with the mass of the Jews who have returned to their land in unbelief. He will guarantee them freedom of worship and promise them his protection in return for their allegiance. After three and a half years, he will break this covenant, stopping the sacrifices the Jews are again performing in a restored temple. His own image will be set up in their temple to be worshiped. This is the "abomination of desolation" to which our Lord later referred in Matthew 24:15 (see also II Thess. 2:4; Rev. 13:14-15). Abominations refer to horrible things and the expression is frequently used in the Old Testament for heathen idols (see, e.g., Deut. 27:15; 32:16; II Kings 23:13).

This conduct of the Antichrist is to continue "even to the consummation"—a reference to the return of the Lord Jesus at which time He will overthrow this beast-king. Then shall "that determined be poured upon the desolator"[8]—a reference to the Antichrist, if this alternate reading is correct. If "desolate" is the proper translation, the word has reference to Israel, and indicates that they will be allowed to suffer until that determined by God has been poured upon them.

Some expositors have thought that this closing verse of chapter 9 refers not to Antichrist, but to Christ and the new covenant in His blood.[9] That cannot be, for His is an everlasting covenant (Heb. 13:20), not a seven-year one.

[8]Scofield, *ibid.*; also Jamieson, Fausset and Brown, *Commentary*, IV, 438.
[9]Biederwolf, p. 223.

Also it was not His people who destroyed Jerusalem and the temple.

This view would also involve the idea that the seventieth "week" of years followed consecutively the sixty-nine "weeks." "Edward J. Young, amillennial in his theology, ... frankly admits that the seven plus sixty-two weeks come to an end before the death of Christ, and maintains that the death of Christ and the destruction of Jerusalem described in verse 26 take place in the seventieth week."[10] But such a view is manifestly untenable. The destruction of Jerusalem took place in A.D. 70. Regardless of some difference of opinion as to the exact year when Christ died, it was obviously in the A.D. 30's and by no stretch of the imagination could His death and the destruction of Jerusalem be forced into the same heptad of years, without utterly destroying the time element of the prophecy, which has previously been so accurate and literal. Also it would indeed take wishful thinking to convince oneself that the five objectives of verse 24 were totally fulfilled long, long ago, though some have claimed this to be so. No, this prophecy concerning the final "week" of the seventy has not yet been fulfilled, but still lies within the future. In due time it will take place, for God has spoken, and He cannot lie (Titus 1:2).

[10]Robert D. Culver, *Daniel and the Latter Days*, p. 149. See his extensive and enlightening discussion of this whole subject (pp. 135-60).

10

THE VISION OF THE GLORY
OF GOD
(10:1-21)

<small>Vision of the Preincarnate Christ</small> (10:1-9)

CHAPTERS 10-12 all record one vision. The introduction is
given in chapter 10. The main body of the prophecy is to
be found in chapter 11. Chapter 12 contains the epilogue.
This vision took place during "the third year of Cyrus king
of Persia." By comparison with Daniel 1:21 it seems likely
that Daniel retired from public service when he was around
eighty years of age, after Cyrus had reigned for one year.
This closing vision was granted to him two years later,
shortly before his death. He carefully affirmed, "And the
thing was true." Many years later, after having been given
a similar vision, the Apostle John was assured: "These say-
ings are faithful and true: and the Lord God of the holy
prophets sent his angel to shew unto his servants the things
which must shortly be done" (Rev. 22:6). God has set His
seal to it that these prophecies will surely be fulfilled. However Daniel states that "the time appointed was long." The
fulfillment of much of Daniel's vision was to take place in

the far distant future. With regard to previous visions, Daniel frankly reveals himself as doubtful concerning the interpretation. About this one he affirms that he "had understanding of the vision."

Daniel's experience took place "in the four and twentieth day of the first month" (v. 4). By comparison with Exodus 12:18 it will be seen that this was just following the time for the Feast of Unleavened Bread, which came immediately after the Passover. The Passover speaks of salvation through the blood; the Feast of Unleavened Bread portrays the holy life that should follow salvation (I Cor. 5:6-8). During this period the Israelites were to mortify the flesh by partaking of unleavened bread for one week. Daniel extended the time to three weeks, also abstaining from flesh and wine, as well as from anointing himself with unguents (a Persian custom).[1] He was evidently mourning—there was sadness in his heart. Two years prior to this time, Cyrus had permitted the Jews to return to Jerusalem (Ezra 1:1-4). But only a minority had taken advantage of this opportunity, and these were far from prosperous, largely due to vigorous opposition from the Samaritans (Ezra 4:1-5). No doubt this depressed condition of the remnant accounted for Daniel's mourning.

Three days after this fast was completed, Daniel, while standing beside the great river Hiddekel (ancient name for the Tigris), saw a glorious vision. His vision was of a Person whose description is quite reminiscent of that of Christ as John saw Him on the Isle of Patmos (Rev. 1). The one Daniel saw must have been the preincarnate Christ, for it seems that the terms used in verses 5-6 could

---

[1]"The Persians largely used unguents" (Jamieson, Fausset and Brown, IV, 440).

fit no other. Because of verse 13, some have identified the person as a mighty angel, but more likely the one speaking there is another personage altogether.

Those present with Daniel did not perceive the actual appearance that Daniel saw, but they did feel that a supernatural presence was near and, being frightened, fled away. This is quite similar to what happened centuries later when Saul of Tarsus saw the risen Lord (Acts 22:9).

As for Daniel himself, he became completely without strength. Though undoubtedly one of the best men to walk this earth, in the presence of the Son of God he acknowledged, "My comeliness was turned in me into corruption." When men truly see the Lord, it never has the effect upon them of causing them to boast of their own righteousness. They rather realize that all their righteousnesses are as "filthy rags" before Him (Isa. 64:6).

Overcome by the glory of the Lord, the prophet fell in a stupor to the ground. In a trancelike condition, he was yet conscious of the Lord's voice speaking.

ANGELIC MINISTRY (10:10-14)

A hand touched Daniel, raising him up. This hand was evidently that of an angel, probably Gabriel who had interpreted other visions for the prophet. As Gabriel had done (9:23), this angel spoke of Daniel as "greatly beloved." With this encouragement and strengthening, the aged man of God, though still trembling, stood upright on his feet. The angel then made it clear that from the very beginning of the period of fasting, when Daniel had first begun to pray to God, his words had been heard and the answer sent. But strange as it may seem, this angelic being, commissioned to minister to Daniel and to reveal to him a new prophecy, was delayed no less than three weeks due to the opposition of one whom he called "the prince of the kingdom of Persia." Surely this could not have been a mere human being. No earthly prince could withstand a mighty angel. The expression must refer to an evil angel, directed by Satan to tempt and influence the kings of Persia. This whole passage is a significant commentary on Ephesians 6:11-12: "Put on the whole armor of God, that you may be able to stand against the wiles of the devil. For we are not contending against flesh and blood, but against the principalities, against the powers, against the world rulers of this present darkness, against the spiritual hosts of wickedness in the heavenly places" (RSV). The various titles used in these verses obviously refer to Satan's hierarchy of evil spirits.

Eventually the good angel was reinforced and thus won the victory. Michael, called in the New Testament "the archangel," came to his assistance. Later in this same vision Michael is called "the great prince which standeth for the children of thy [Daniel's] people" (12:1). Michael has been divinely appointed the guardian angel of Israel.

When Gabriel (if it be he) said: "I remained there [or, I was detained there][2] with the kings of Persia," he seemed to allude to further evil spirits who had opposed him.

After this explanation, the angel indicated to Daniel that the prophecy about to be given related to the affairs of Israel in the distant future, particularly to the latter (or last)[3] days—an expression used for the time of the second coming of Christ and the period just preceding it.

[2]Jamieson, Fausset and Brown, *Commentary*, IV, 441.
[3]Same Hebrew word rendered "last" in Gen. 49:1; Isa. 2:2; Micah 4:1.

DIVINE MINISTRY (10:15-17)

Overcome by weakness once again, Daniel fell to the ground. The Lord graciously ministered to him. Unable to speak until the Lord had opened his lips, Daniel indicated that he was still too weak to carry on a conversation.

INTRODUCTION TO THE FINAL PROPHECY
(10:18-21)

Once more the Lord sent the angel to strengthen Daniel and to give him the further revelation. After this empowering, Daniel was sufficiently recovered to proceed. Gabriel then spoke of a second "prince," this time of "Grecia." This reference is to another evil spirit, one evidently assigned to the land of Greece. These intimations reveal that Satan has his evil angels assigned to the various nations of the earth. His forces are well organized.

Gabriel promised that before he continued this spiritual conflict, he would show the prophet that which was noted in "the Scriptures of truth." This is not an allusion to the Bible, for these matters had not yet been written in an earthly book. The reference is rather to a heavenly record, kept by God Himself, showing what He has ordained to come to pass. Certain of these matters He has graciously revealed to us, and so our Bible, containing these revelations, can also appropriately be called the Scriptures of truth.

In these affairs of Israel, the angel stated: "There is none that holdeth with me in these things, but Michael your prince." It appears that to Gabriel and Michael alone is committed the task of protecting Israel against the demonic powers of Satan's world-system, though the reason for this is an unexplained mystery.

11

PROPHECIES CONCERNING PERSIA, GRECIA AND THE TIME OF THE END

(11:1-45)

THIS CHAPTER contains a marvelously detailed prophecy of events in relation to Israel which were to follow for the next three hundred years. A comparison with secular history provides a striking confirmation of the divine inspiration of Scripture.[1]

PROPHECIES CONCERNING PERSIA (11:1-2)

Though this entire prophecy was given during the third year of Cyrus (10:1), Gabriel first mentioned an earlier time when he had secretly confirmed and strengthened Darius, in the latter's first year. This evidently took place about the time Daniel was cast into the lions' den, but its significance is obscure. With verse 2 the actual prediction began. Three kings were yet to reign in Persia. These three proved to be Cambyses, Pseudo-Smerdis and Darius Hys-

---

[1]The various events of "secular" history which are cited in the present chapter are drawn from Herodotus, Josephus and various modern authorities who recount the history of this period. The facts can easily be verified by consulting such writers.

taspes. Cambyses, the son of Cyrus, had his younger brother Smerdis assassinated. While Cambyses was away on an expedition to Egypt, an impostor who bore a likeness to Smerdis declared himself king. Cambyses started home to deal with this "Pseudo-Smerdis," but died on the way. The impostor reigned seven months before meeting his own death. Then the son-in-law of Cyrus, Darius Hystaspes, became monarch.[2]

Gabriel then spoke of a fourth who was to be "far richer than them all." In fulfillment, this was Xerxes (apparently the Ahasuerus of Esther).[3] With an army of 2,641,000 he crossed the Hellespont and invaded Greece. It was predicted that he would "stir up all against the realm of Grecia." He did indeed spend four years gathering his army, but its very size defeated him and he was driven back into Asia, being defeated at the crucial battle of Salamis (480 b.c.). The Greeks never forgot this aggression. For long they thirsted for a revenge that they finally achieved.

Prophecies Concerning Grecia (11:3-4)

In due time a "mighty king" did "stand up"—Alexander the Great (356-323 b.c.). This mighty king did indeed "rule with great dominion" and he conquered Persia. The prophecy indicates, however, that at the zenith of the power of this ruler, "his kingdom shall be broken, and shall be divided toward the four winds of heaven; and not to his posterity." Although Alexander had two sons, Hercules and Alexander II, neither reigned on his throne. Both were slain, one before and one after his father. After the Battle of Ipsus (301 b.c.) Alexander's kingdom was divided be-

[2]For the full story, see Herodotus, *The Persian Wars*, III. 61-79.
[3]G. Coleman Luck, *Ezra and Nehemiah*, p. 50.

tween his four leading generals. From this point on, the prophecy concerns two of these four rulers and their successors. "The king of the south" is a reference to the ruler of Egypt, Ptolemy Lagus, and his successors. "The king of the north" refers to the ruler of Syria, Seleucus, and those who followed him. The terms south and north are used with regard to Israel, Egypt being south and Syria north of that land.

PROPHECIES CONCERNING TWO BRANCHES OF THE DIVIDED GREEK EMPIRE: SYRIA AND EGYPT (11:5-35)

These verses cover prophetically a period of about 200 years, and have to do with the wars of the Seleucidae and the Ptolemies. These dynasties waged almost constant warfare with each other. Palestine, lying between the two, was frequently the battleground. It is important to remember that this section covers a long portion of time, and the "king of the south" and the "king of the north" throughout the passage are not the same individuals.

The word *one* in verse 5 is not in the original text and should be omitted. The statement is that "the king of the south shall be strong, and of his princes," that is, of Alexander's princes. Ptolemy Lagus, the first "king of the south," was indeed in the beginning stronger than Seleucus, the original "king of the north." This is the meaning of the expression "He shall be strong above him" (v. 5). Seleucus however later became the stronger when he added Babylonia and Media to his domain.

Verse 6 predicts a time "in the end of years" when the kings of these two domains "shall join themselves together," with the king of Syria marrying the daughter of the king of Egypt. Antiochus Theos (285-247 B.C.), the third king of

Syria, divorced his own wife Laodice to marry Berenice, daughter of Ptolemy Philadelphus. Later Laodice stirred up her friends against the king, and caused Berenice and her attendants to be put to death. Antiochus reinstated Laodice who shortly poisoned him too, and brought her son Seleucus Callinicus to the throne.

Verse 7 indicates that from "a branch of her [Berenice's] roots" one will come who will prevail against the king of the north. Ptolemy Euergetes, brother of Berenice, defeated Callinicus. News of sedition in Egypt caused Euergetes to hasten back to Egypt, carrying captives (v. 8). Callinicus later died of a fall from a horse, so Euergetes did "continue more years," actually reigning four years longer than the Syrian king. However he did not again return to Syria (v. 9).

Verse 10 prophesies that the sons of the king of Syria (Callinicus) "shall be stirred up." These sons were Seleucus Ceraunus and Antiochus the Great. They assembled an army to avenge themselves on the Egyptians. But Ceraunus died less than two years later, leaving his brother sole ruler. Antiochus the Great became a noted king, one of his exploits being to lead an army of 75,000 against Egypt. But surprisingly Ptolemy Philopater, an indolent, wicked man, defeated Antiochus at the Battle of Raphia with a great slaughter (v. 11). Too lethargic to follow up his victory, however, he concluded an ignoble peace with Antiochus (v. 12).

Antiochus formed an alliance with Philip III of Macedon (v. 13) and also sought help of the Jews (v. 14). The godly refused to join his army, but the apostates ("the robbers of thy people") helped him. However it was predicted that "they shall fall," and they did not achieve the hoped-for independence of Judaea.

Antiochus the Great utterly routed the Egyptian forces (v. 15). He stood in "the glorious land," Palestine; and as prophesied it was "in his power" according to the Berkeley Version, not "consumed" as in the Authorized Version. In order to further control Egypt, Antiochus gave his daughter Cleopatra to Ptolemy Epiphanes, but it proved true that "she shall not stand on his side, neither be for him" (v. 17). She supported her husband rather than her father.

Antiochus next determined to conquer Greece. "The isles" (v. 18) of the Aegean Sea were taken, and he crossed the Hellespont, but Greece was now allied with the rising power of Rome. The Roman Senate commissioned Lucius Scipio Asiaticus to go for relief. He utterly routed Antiochus at Magnesia in 190 B.C.

Antiochus, now humbled, turned back (v. 19). But attempting to plunder the temple of Jupiter at Elymais (near Shushan)—perhaps to pay Roman tribute—he and his soldiers were slain by an angry populace. He was succeeded by his son Seleucus Philopater. The latter was "a raiser of taxes" (v. 20), in order to obtain the tribute to pay Rome. He sent Heliodorus to Jerusalem to plunder the temple there. Shortly afterward Heliodorus treacherously slew his master.

Verses 21-35 center around Antiochus Epiphanes, already mentioned in connection with chapter 8. He has been called the Antichrist of the Old Testament period. This king hated Israel and Jehovah. His courtiers called him *epiphanes*—"the splendid"—but some wit of the day suggested that one letter of his name be changed to make it *epimanes*—"the madman." This "vile person" (v. 21) first made a league with the Jews and with Egypt, but later broke his covenant. Verses 22-24 picture his treachery; he fought against Egypt and Ptolemy Philometer (v. 25). When Ptolemy's own sons and servants betrayed him, he was defeated (v. 26). He and Antiochus then met and made promises which neither intended to keep (v. 27). The Jews meantime heard an erroneous report that Antiochus was killed. This caused them great rejoicing. Antiochus, learning of this, on his way home marched against Jerusalem, sacking it with great cruelty (v. 28).

The Jews appealed to Rome for help. Rome responded and sent an army while Antiochus was marching against the Jewish forces, led by the Maccabees (v. 29). Antiochus submitted to Rome and promised to keep the peace, but as soon as the legions were gone he "had indignation" (v. 30) and broke his promises. Traitorous Jews ("them that forsake the covenant") assisted him. He desecrated the temple (v. 31), setting up a statue of Jupiter there (which he identified with himself). He stopped the service of Jehovah, decreeing that he alone should be worshiped. He even sacrificed a sow on the altar. The faithful fought against him, led by a heroic family called the Maccabees, but thousands of them were slaughtered. His defiling of the temple was an "abomination that maketh desolate," and a foreshadowing of a similar event, yet future, spoken of by Daniel (12:11) and much later by the Lord Jesus Christ (Matt. 24:15). The length of Antiochus' desecration had already been foretold in Daniel 8:14.

Verses 32-35 graphically picture conditions among the Jews during the troublous times of Antiochus' reign. But in verse 35 "the time of the end" is mentioned. Then immediately and suddenly the vision passed over "the great parenthesis" and jumped to the end times and the Antichrist yet to come, with a detailed description of this evil man and his doings.

THE TIME OF THE END—THE ANTICHRIST
(11:36-45)

Verses 36-39 present the same character spoken of in Daniel 7:8; 9:26 In those chapters he was called the "little horn," "the prince that shall come." Here he is characterized as the willful king—"the king shall do according to his will" (v. 36). His character is first described, then the chapter closes with an account of events during his struggles in the last days.

Even as Lucifer did originally (Isa. 14:13-14), this man will place his will as supreme, even against that of God Himself. He will be the superlative example of self-glorification which this world has produced—the exact opposite of the Christian ideal. He will even claim divine honors for himself. "He shall exalt himself, and magnify himself above every god." Furthermore he will utter marvelous things (that is, of blasphemy) against the Lord Jehovah, "the God of gods." Strangely enough, he will thrive in his impious course for a time—"till the indignation be accomplished"; in other words, until God's indignation against Israel because of their sins be completed, until "the time of Jacob's trouble" (Jer. 30:7) has been finished.

Because of the statement that he will not "regard the God of his fathers" (v. 37), some commentators have judged that the Antichrist will be an apostate Jew, and it has been argued that "the desire of women" refers to the desire of Jewish women to bear the Messiah. In view of the fact that this wicked ruler is to be the head of a reconstituted Roman Empire, and that he will turn against the Jews, breaking his covenant with them, it seems more reasonable to conclude that he will be an apostate Christian. In the expression "the God of his fathers," the Hebrew word translated "God" is *Elohim,* which is often and properly translated "gods." The simple thought seems to be no more than that he will have no regard for any type of religion practiced by his ancestors. That he has no concern for "the desire of women" can most naturally be taken as meaning that he cares nothing for women or their desires. Adolph Hitler was for a long time reputed to be a man of this sort. It is evident that there will be nothing romantic or sentimental about the Antichrist. He will be a man utterly without religion—he will not "regard any god." He will be completely intent on magnifying and exalting himself as world-ruler—"he shall magnify himself above all." This ambition is his only love.

The only god he will honor is "the god of forces," or "fortresses" (ASV). He serves only the "god" of military might and power. After the earlier statement that he does not "regard any god" (v. 37), it is rather surprising to read that "a god whom his fathers knew not shall he honor" (v. 38), but could not this be a reference to himself? He claims divine honors for himself and amasses wealth and power for himself alone. He himself then is the "strange god whom he shall acknowledge and increase with glory" (v. 39).

Verses 40-45 relate some of the events of the last days in which the willful king and other personages figure. These events are very significantly said to occur "at the time of the end" (v. 40). In the light of this expression, how could this passage refer to Antiochus Epiphanes, Nero, or some former pope, as certain commentators have imagined? It should be carefully observed that these closing verses of chapter 11 present to the reader three persons of the "last days"—the willful king (the Antichrist), the "king of the south" (the ruler then controlling Egypt), and the "king of the north" (the ruler then controlling Syria). Against Antichrist the latter two kings come with mighty armies, but it is apparent that they meet with little success in their struggles with him. As for Antichrist, he is almost completely victorious, although a few countries do not come under his power.

Eventually evil tidings reach him from two directions—of great forces being gathered against him (v. 44). "Out of the east" would suggest Oriental power, and "out of the north," Russia. These tidings merely cause an increase in the fury of his persecutions: "Therefore he shall go forth with great fury to destroy, and utterly to make away many." He will establish his headquarters at Jerusalem: "He shall plant the tabernacles of his palace between the seas in the glorious holy mountain" (v. 45). The "seas" are the Mediterranean and Dead seas. The "glorious holy mountain" is Mount Zion. Another translation suggests that his palace will be a bit farther west between the Mediterranean and Mount Zion: "He shall plant the tents of his palace between the sea, and the glorious holy mountain" (ASV). But in spite of his irresistible power, at the appointed time his doom will come, and when that moment arrives no one will be able to succor him. "Yet he shall come to his end, and none shall help him."

12

THE GREAT TRIBULATION AND
THE RESURRECTION
(12:1-13)

THE GREAT TRIBULATION (12:1)

OPENING WITH THE WORDS "and at that time," this chapter continues without pause the thought of chapter 11. At the time of the willful king's ascendancy, the archangel Michael "shall stand up"; that is, he shall exert himself on behalf of the people of Israel. (This statement should be carefully compared with the teaching of Rev. 12.) The reason why the period just before the Lord's return to reign is called the great tribulation is here explained. "There shall be a time of trouble, such as never was since there was a nation even to that same time." When we think of some of the awful things that have happened on this earth in both ancient and modern times, this statement becomes more meaningful and indeed solemnizes our hearts. (Do not fail to observe the description which Christ gave of this same period in Matt. 24:15-22.)

From this time of trouble there shall however come deliverance for Daniel's people, the Jews, but not for each individual. The deliverance will extend to "every one that shall be found written in the book." The book is the Lamb's book of life, in which are recorded God's own (Rev. 13:8).

THE RESURRECTION (12:2-3)

The two resurrections are here clearly distinguished, though the time relation between them is not brought forth. The New Testament reveals that the resurrection of the saved will take place first, so that they may reign with Christ during the millennial kingdom (Rev. 20:6). A thousand years later comes the final resurrection—this time of the unsaved, who are judged and cast into the lake of fire (Rev. 20:7, 12-15). When the Lord "makes up his jewels" (Mal. 3:17), those who were truly wise—those who have won souls—"shall shine as the brightness of the firmament." Such may now be ignored by the world, but the true wisdom of serving God will be made clear at that future day.

EPILOGUE (12:4-13)

Daniel was told to "seal the book, even to the time of the end." This makes it clear that its prophecies would not be completely understood for many years to come after Daniel's day. In Revelation 22:10 the Apostle John is told not to seal his book since "the time is at hand." The present age not being directly foretold in the Old Testament, now that we have come to it, the time of the end is considered imminent and the book is now unsealed. John's Revelation is the key to Daniel's prophecy. Some have taken the expression "Many shall run to and fro, and knowledge shall be increased" to refer to great advances in transportation and science in our own day. More likely the thought is that "many shall run to and fro" through this book of Daniel, and knowledge of it shall be increased.[1]

To close the vision, Daniel saw two other angels and the "man clothed in linen" (the preincarnate Christ of 10:6). The angels inquired as to how long these wonderful events (of the great tribulation) should last. The answer was for three and a half years ("time, times, and a half"). Once again the last half of Daniel's seventieth week is in view—the intensive period of persecution. These three and a half years which are to follow the breaking of the beast-king's covenant are a time of extreme affliction.

Daniel did not understand, and inquired for further enlightenment (v. 8). He was told that no more information would be given him (v. 9). A word was offered him, however, regarding conditions that would in general exist from his own day to the coming of Christ in glory: "Many shall be purified, and made white, and tried; but the wicked shall do wickedly: and none of the wicked shall understand; but the wise shall understand" (v. 10). God grant that each person who reads these words may be among "the wise" who "shall understand"!

Some further figures of significance were granted to Daniel. This time "days" were used. "The abomination of desolation" is to be followed by 1,290 days. This comes to exactly three and a half years plus one month (using prophetic years of 360 days). The exact purpose of this extra month is not stated. It may perhaps be the time taken off "for the elect's sake" (Matt. 24:22). Possibly during

[1]"The word means to run about in order to search out and investigate. It cannot therefore mean mere increase of travel. It might mean travel for a purpose, the result of which is the increase of knowledge, but we prefer rather the meaning of to and fro in the sense of searching, scrutinizing the prophecy as a result of which knowledge of it will be increased" (William Edward Biederwolf, *The Millennium Bible*, p. 240).

this month, the rebels will be purged from Israel (Ezek. 20:33-38). It is however clearly stated that the one who continues on for an additional month and a half longer will be "blessed"—because Christ will then be reigning in His full glory on this old earth.

As the revelation ended, Daniel was told to go his way (v. 13). He was soon going to be with his Lord, but he was promised a blessed resurrection "at the end of the days." Then he will "stand in . . . [his] lot." This is true of all others who trust in Christ. If we suffer with Him now, we will reign with Him then (II Tim. 1:12). "He which testifieth these things saith, Surely I come quickly. Amen. Even so, come, Lord Jesus. The grace of our Lord Jesus Christ be with you all. Amen" (Rev. 22:20-21).

BIBLIOGRAPHY

ANDERSON, SIR ROBERT. *The Coming Prince*. Grand Rapids: Kregel, 1954.

ANGUS, JOSEPH. *The Bible Handbook*. Grand Rapids: Zondervan, 1952.

ARCHER, GLEASON L., JR. *A Survey of Old Testament Introduction*. Chicago: Moody, 1964.

BIEDERWOLF, WILLIAM EDWARD. *The Millennium Bible*. Grand Rapids: Baker, 1964.

CULVER, ROBERT D. *Daniel and the Latter Days*. Chicago: Moody, 1965.

FAIRBAIRN, PATRICK. *Imperial Standard Bible Encyclopedia*. Grand Rapids: Zondervan, 1957.

GAEBELEIN, A. C. *The Prophet Daniel*. Grand Rapids: Kregel, 1955.

GESENIUS, WILLIAM. *Hebrew and Chaldee Lexicon to the Old Testament Scriptures*. Grand Rapids: Eerdmans, 1949.

HALEY, JOHN W. *An Examination of the Alleged Discrepancies of the Bible*. Nashville: B. C. Goodpasture, 1951.

HARTILL, S. EDWIN. *Biblical Hermeneutics*. 10th ed.; Grand Rapids: Zondervan, 1960.

HENRY, MATTHEW. *Commentary on the Whole Bible*. Grand Rapids: Zondervan, 1961.

HERODOTUS. *The Persian Wars*. Trans. George Rawlinson. New York: Modern Library, n.d.

IRONSIDE, H. A. *The Great Parenthesis*. New York: Loizeaux, 1943.

———. *Lectures on Daniel the Prophet*. New York: Loizeaux, 1920.

JAMIESON, ROBERT; FAUSSET, A. R.; AND BROWN, DAVID. *A Commentary on the Old and New Testaments*. Grand Rapids: Eerdmans, 1948.

JOSEPHUS, FLAVIUS. *Works*. Philadelphia: Winston, n.d.

KEIL, C. F. *Biblical Commentary on the Book of Daniel*. Grand Rapids: Eerdmans, 1949.

LARKIN, CLARENCE. *The Book of Daniel*. Philadelphia: Larkin, 1953.

LUCK, G. COLEMAN. *Ezra and Nehemiah*. Chicago: Moody, 1961.

MACLAREN, ALEXANDER. *Expositions of Holy Scripture*. Grand Rapids: Eerdmans, 1944.

METZGER, BRUCE M. (ed.). *The Oxford Annotated Apocrypha*. New York: Oxford U., 1965.

MORGAN, G. CAMPBELL. *Living Messages of the Books of the Bible, Old Testament*. New York: Revell, 1912.

MORSE, JOSEPH L. (ed.). *Universal Standard Encyclopaedia*. New York: Funk & Wagnalls, 1954.

ORR, JAMES (ed.). *International Standard Bible Encyclopaedia*. Grand Rapids: Eerdmans, 1949.

OWEN, G. FREDERICK. *Archaeology and the Bible*. Westwood, N.J.: Revell, 1961.

PETTINGILL, WILLIAM L. *Simple Studies in Daniel*. Philadelphia: Phila. School of Bible, 1920.

PFEIFFER, CHARLES F. (ed.). *The Biblical World*. Grand Rapids: Baker, 1966.

SCOFIELD, C. I. *The Scofield Reference Bible*. New York: Oxford U., 1945.

SPENCE, H. D. M., AND EXELL, JOSEPH S. (eds.). *Pulpit Commentary*. New York: Funk & Wagnalls, n.d.

TALBOT, LOUIS T. *The Prophecy of Daniel in the Light of Past, Present, and Future Events.* Wheaton: Van Kampen, 1954.

UNGER, MERRILL F. *Unger's Bible Dictionary.* Chicago: Moody, 1957.

VINE, W. E. *Expository Dictionary of New Testament Words.* Westwood, N. J.: Revell, n.d.

WHITCOMB, JOHN C. *Darius the Mede.* Grand Rapids: Baker, 1959.

YOUNG, ROBERT. *Analytical Concordance to the Bible.* New York: Funk & Wagnalls, 1893.